Walking in Victory

A Spiritual, Cognitive-Behavioral Workbook

by Robert L. Brown

Walking In Victory

Copyright © 2015 by Robert L. Brown.

All rights reserved.

No part of this book may be reproduced or transmitted in any form or by any means, electronic or mechanical, including photocopying, recording, or by any information storage and retrieval system known or to be invented, without permission, in writing from the publisher. Portions of this book have been adapted from *How to Escape Your Prison* (© 1988) by permission.

> Eagle Wing Books, Inc.
> P.O. Box 9972
> Memphis, TN 38190
>
> www.ccimrt.com

All Scripture quotations, unless otherwise indicated, are taken from the HOLY BIBLE, NEW INTERNATIONAL VERSION® (NIV®); Copyright © 1973, 1978, 1984 by International Bible Society. Used by permission of Zondervan. All rights reserved.

Scripture quotations marked (TLB) are taken from The Living Bible copyright © 1971. Used by permission of Tyndale House Publishers, Inc., Carol Stream, Illinois 60188. All rights reserved.

Scripture taken from the International Children's Bible®; Copyright © 1986, 1988, 1999 by Thomas Nelson, Inc. Used by permission. All rights reserved. Other scripture quotes are from the KJV.

Clipart and photos from Corel, Nova Development, Bigstock Photo, & Robert Brown.

All rights reserved. Published July 2015.

ISBN 10: 0940829428
ISBN 13: 978-0-940829-42-8

Acknowledgements

I would like to say thank you to all of those at the first meeting in Memphis, which launched this workbook. You were all so encouraging.

John and Jo Walt
Fred Hackl
Laura Gilbeath
Ken Robinson, Ed. D.
Meli Brown

I want to express my deepest gratitude to Dr. Kenneth D. Robinson and Dr. Gregory L. Little, co-developers of Moral Reconation Therapy (MRT™). Thank you for the opportunity to bring this workbook into reality and your support throughout the process.

I also want to thank Traci McConnell for her valuable proofreading and editing skills.

Special thanks to my wife, Meli, and my sons: Cris and Bobby. Without your love and support I am not sure any of this would have been possible.

And I thank God for each day that I have, to learn to better walk in His story for me, and His love for all.

Bob Brown, July, 2015

The Victory Ladder
Facilitator Checklist & Table of Contents

Client Name: _____

	Page	Date Completed	Facilitator Initials

Chapter One: 1
    Preface (Counselor)
    Effects of Addiction (Counselor)

Chapter Two: 11
    Laying a Foundation (Counselor)
    The Problem of Addiction (Counselor)

Chapter Three: 19
    Step One: Part One (Counselor)
    Road of Life (Group)
    Life Story (Group)

Chapter Four: 31
    Step One: Part Two (Counselor)
    Life Cross (Group)
    Life wheel (Group)
    Testimony (Group)

Chapter Five: 43
    Step Two (Counselor)
    Your Decision (Group)
    Share with Others (Group)

Chapter Six: 51
    Step Three (Counselor)
    Knowing God (Group)
    Truth about God (Group)
    Who Am I (Group)

Chapter Seven: 69
- Step Four (Counselor)
- Group Discussions (Counselor)
- 10 Hours of Helping Others (Counselor)
- Important Relationships (Counselor)
- With God/Without God (Group)
- Life Wheel (Group)
- Trading Places (Group)

Chapter Eight: 87
- Step Five (Counselor)
- One Year to Live (Counselor)
- Five Years to Live (Counselor)
- Ten Years to Live (Counselor)
- Master Vision Plan (Counselor)
- Action Plan (Counselor)

Chapter Nine: 101
- Step Six (Counselor)
- Update Action Plan (Counselor)
- 10 Hours of Helping Others (Counselor)
- Trading Places (Group)
- Moral Assessment (Counselor)
- My 5 Biggest Problem (Counselor)

Chapter Ten: 115
- Step Seven (Counselor)
- Important Relationships (Counselor)
- Summary of Things Learned in Steps (Group)

Chapter Eleven: 123
- Step Eight (Counselor)
- With God/ Without God (Group)

Chapter Twelve: 133
- Step Nine (Counselor)
- Your Encouragement to Others (Group)

The Victory Ladder

Step 9—*Walking in Victory*—Walk the Walk & Grace
This is the top rung of the Victory Ladder. Here, you talk the talk and walk the walk. Here is where you walk in the grace of God. You glorify God in all that you do, *Walking in Love*.

Step 8—*Love*—Choosing Moral Goals & Reality
At this rung in the journey to victory you add love to what you think and what you do. All is placed in God's hands.

Step 7—*Kindness*—Keeping Moral Commitments—Diligence
Love like this is not a feeling but a decision made to meet other's needs. You extend kindness to all in your life and also to yourself.

Step 6—*Godliness*—Commitment to Change—Vulnerability
You have moved to a new way of life and by setting goals, you made yourself vulnerable. Here, you add godliness to your walk by living the way God wants you to live.

Step 5—*Perseverance*—Identity Formation—Uncommitted
This rung on the ladder concerns finding your calling, formulating your vision, and establishing the right goals for yourself. Then, it concerns persistence in keeping to your goals.

Step 4—*Self-Control*—Helping Others & Healing Damaged Relationships—Wounded
Realizing that you have been the problem in your life, you begin to make better choices: to repair damaged relationships and be obedient to God's Word. Here, you reach out to others to share the love of Christ through your life.

Step 3—*Knowledge*—Awareness—Disobedience
In this Step on the ladder, you become aware of who God is and who you are. You become aware that you have been living life the wrong way and choose to to renew your mind and life and be transformed.

Step 2—*Goodness*—Acceptance—Disobedience
To continue the climb on the Victory Ladder, out of the bondage of your past, you have to be willing to let go of the path you previously chose and accept the path God has for you. Without God, you are powerless to save yourself.

Step 1—*Faith*—Trust & Honesty—Alienation
The journey of the Victory Ladder began with the fall of mankind in the garden. We don't like the way things are, how we feel, or who we are. We want the world to be what we want it to be and make choices to make it that way. We do not seek God's way for us. We need to ask God, "what should we do?"

Chapter 1
PREFACE &
The Effects of Addiction

One day while at work I was sitting in the waiting area. It was a slow day, as I didn't have many clients to see or any pressing needs as director of a counseling center. All was quiet, even the employees seemed not to need my attention. I began to ponder, "What have I been doing with my life?" "Have I been fulfilling the desires of my heart?" I believed that God had called me to the ministry.

I had left the Air Force and entered Oral Roberts University to develop the gifts God had given me. I studied to be a pastor with the hopes of pastoring a church someday. I completed my training, graduated with a Bachelors' Degree in Pastoral Care and Church Administration with a minor in Counseling. I then went on to complete a Masters' Degree in Christian Counseling.

I had been working in an alcohol and drug outpatient treatment center for about three years and was about 45 years old at the time. I was hired as a full-time counselor and within one year became the Executive Director. Things were going well.

However, as I sat there, I continued to reflect back over my life and all the "living" I had experienced. As I looked back through the years I realized that I had done a lot of "living." I had made it through my youth, finished high school, served over twelve years in the military, traveled overseas, met my wife, and raised two children. Despite years of partying and drinking, I had completed college and was enjoying life.

I then began to think, "I am now forty-five." I subtracted the first ten years of my life due to the fact I was just growing up. That left thirty-five years of "living." Looking ahead, I figured I could easily live another thirty-five years. I thought, "I have another whole lifetime in front of me." Most of the first thirty years were just me doing what I wanted, not much of God was in the picture. I wondered about the idea that I now had the Creator of the Universe, the Almighty God living inside of me.

Then, the questions came. What would my life be like if I truly surrendered myself to God, stopped doing it my way, stopped writing my own story and started living in the story God had written for me? What could the next thirty-five years be like?

Perhaps, you have wondered what your life is really about. What have you done with your life? Why haven't you been able to reach your goals, your full potential? Where has God been all this time? Maybe life has been good to you, you are prosperous. Your family is intact and you feel good about what you've accomplished. But something inside gnaws at you concerning where you are at with God.

You are probably doing all the right things: going to church, tithing, helping others, and maybe you haven't been angry in a long time. You get the idea. However, something is still missing. Maybe the desires of your heart are what are missing. Perhaps it's not about doing all the right things. For so long you've tried, on your own, to do it the right way.

What is missing? Maybe it's more about walking in the grace of God that He provides through His Son, and the life Jesus came to give us.

This workbook is about the journey back to walking in the cool of the day with God. Going back to where we walk in His Grace, where the desires of our hearts are fully alive. The journey of walking in victory begins with faith.

What Does the Bible Say About Addictions?

The Bible has much to say about the effects from the use of alcohol. I know it doesn't mention all the other drugs, but we understand that alcohol is a drug too! So it is not out of context to speak of all drugs when addressing addictions from a biblical perspective. What about other addictions? The process is the same. When sin masters us it must do its work.

This is your first exercise. The facilitator will verify that you have read each reference and may ask questions confirm that you understand.

Effects of Addiction—Blackouts:
(Genesis 19:30-36)

³⁰ Lot and his two daughters left Zoar and settled in the mountains, for he was afraid to stay in Zoar. He and his two daughters lived in a cave.

³¹ One day the older daughter said to the younger, "Our father is old, and there is no man around here to lie with us, as is the custom all over the earth.

³² Let's get our father to drink wine and then lie with him and preserve our family line through our father."

³³ That night they got their father to drink wine, and the older daughter went in and lay with him. He was not aware of it when she lay down or when she got up.

³⁴ The next day the older daughter said to the younger, "Last night I lay with my father. Let's get him to drink wine again tonight, and you go in and lie with him so we can preserve our family line through our father."

³⁵ So they got their father to drink wine that night also, and the younger daughter went and lay with him. Again he was not aware of it when she lay down or when she got up.

³⁶ So both of Lot's daughters became pregnant by their father.

Effects the memory, Job problems, Psychological effects: (Proverbs 31:4-7)

⁴"It is not for kings, O Lemuel— not for kings to drink wine, not for rulers to crave beer, ⁵lest they drink and forget what the law decrees, and deprive all the oppressed of their rights.

⁶Give beer to those who are perishing, wine to those who are in anguish; ⁷let them drink and forget their poverty and remember their misery no more.

Effects decision process, judgment impaired, vomit and disorder: (Isaiah 28:7-8)

⁷And these also stagger from wine and reel from beer: Priests and prophets stagger from beer and are befuddled with wine; they reel from beer, they stagger when seeing visions, they stumble when rendering decisions.

⁸All the tables are covered with vomit and there is not a spot without filth.

Financial problems: (Proverbs 21:17; 23:20-21)

¹⁷He who loves pleasure will become poor; whoever loves wine and oil will never be rich.

²⁰Do not join those who drink too much wine or gorge themselves on meat, ²¹for drunkards and gluttons become poor, and drowsiness clothes them in rags.

Physical, emotional and spiritual breakdown: (Proverbs 23:29-30)

²⁹Who has woe? Who has sorrow? Who has strife? Who has complaints? Who has needless bruises? Who has bloodshot eyes?

³⁰Those who linger over wine, who go to sample bowls of mixed wine.

Spiritual and moral breakdown: (Ephesians 5:18)

¹⁸Do not get drunk on wine, which leads to debauchery. Instead, be filled with the Spirit.

Cravings, addiction: (Proverbs 23:31-35)

³¹Do not gaze at wine when it is red, when it sparkles in the cup, when it goes down smoothly! ³²In the end it bites like a snake and poisons like a viper.

³³Your eyes will see strange sights and your mind imagine confusing things.

³⁴You will be like one sleeping on the high seas, lying on top of the rigging. ³⁵"They hit me," you will say, "but I'm not hurt! They beat me, but I don't feel it! When will I wake up so I can find another drink?"

Forsake others for drugs: (Joel 3:3)

³ They cast lots for my people and traded boys for prostitutes; they sold girls for wine that they might drink.

Self-centeredness of using: (Amos 4:1; 6:3-6)

¹ Hear this word, you cows of Bashan on Mount Samaria, you women who oppress the poor and crush the needy and say to your husbands, "Bring us some drinks!"
³ You put off the evil day and bring near a reign of terror.
⁴ You lie on beds inlaid with ivory and lounge on your couches. You dine on choice lambs and fattened calves.
⁵ You strum away on your harps like David and improvise on musical instruments.
⁶ You drink wine by the bowlful and use the finest lotions, but you do not grieve over the ruin of Joseph.

Progressiveness of disease: (Luke 11:24-26)

²⁴ "When an evil spirit comes out of a man, it goes through arid places seeking rest and does not find it. Then it says, 'I will return to the house I left.'
²⁵ When it arrives, it finds the house swept clean and put in order.
²⁶ Then it goes and takes seven other spirits more wicked than itself, and they go in and live there. And the final condition of that man is worse than the first."

Return to drinking-gets worse: (2 Peter 2:19-22)

¹⁹ They promise them freedom, while they themselves are slaves of depravity—for a man is a slave to whatever has mastered him.
²⁰ If they have escaped the corruption of the world by knowing our Lord and Savior Jesus Christ and are again entangled in it and overcome, they are worse off at the end than they were at the beginning.
²¹ It would have been better for them not to have known the way of righteousness, than to have known it and then to turn their backs on the sacred command that was passed on to them.
²² Of them the proverbs are true: "A dog returns to its vomit," and, "A sow that is washed goes back to her wallowing in the mud."

Cover up of positive character: (Romans 13:13–14)

¹³ Let us behave decently, as in the daytime, not in orgies and drunkenness, not in sexual immorality and debauchery, not in dissension and jealousy.
¹⁴ Rather, clothe yourselves with the Lord Jesus Christ, and do not think about how to gratify the desires of the sinful nature.

Unable to talk to person: (1 Samuel 25:36-38)

36 When Abigail went to Nabal, he was in the house holding a banquet like that of a king. He was in high spirits and very drunk. So she told him nothing until daybreak.

37 Then in the morning, when Nabal was sober, his wife told him all these things, and his heart failed him and he became like a stone.

38 About ten days later, the LORD struck Nabal and he died.

Fetal Alcohol Syndrome: (Judges 13:4-14)

4 Now see to it that you drink no wine or other fermented drink and that you do not eat anything unclean, 5 because you will conceive and give birth to a son. No razor may be used on his head, because the boy is to be a Nazirite, set apart to God from birth, and he will begin the deliverance of Israel from the hands of the Philistines."

6 Then the woman went to her husband and told him, "A man of God came to me. He looked like an angel of God, very awesome. I didn't ask him where he came from, and he didn't tell me his name.

7 But he said to me, 'You will conceive and give birth to a son. Now then, drink no wine or other fermented drink and do not eat anything unclean, because the boy will be a Nazirite of God from birth until the day of his death.'"

8 Then Manoah prayed to the LORD: "O Lord, I beg you, let the man of God you sent to us come again to teach us how to bring up the boy who is to be born."

9 God heard Manoah, and the angel of God came again to the woman while she was out in the field; but her husband Manoah was not with her.

10 The woman hurried to tell her husband, "He's here! The man who appeared to me the other day!"

11 Manoah got up and followed his wife. When he came to the man, he said, "Are you the one who talked to my wife?" "I am," he said.

12 So Manoah asked him, "When your words are fulfilled, what is to be the rule for the boy's life and work?"

13 The angel of the LORD answered, "Your wife must do all that I have told her.

14 She must not eat anything that comes from the grapevine, nor drink any wine or other fermented drink nor eat anything unclean. She must do everything I have commanded her."

Addiction: (Titus 2:3)

3 Likewise, teach the older women to be reverent in the way they live, not to be slanderers or addicted to much wine, but to teach what is good.

Insanity of the disease: (Isaiah 56:12)

12 "Come," each one cries, "let me get wine! Let us drink our fill of beer! And tomorrow will be like today, or even far better."

BIBLE STUDY

Throughout this workbook you will be required to look up various Scripture references and write them in the space provided. The reason you must look up and write the Scripture referenced is to help you become familiar with the Bible and what the Word of God says. If you need to, feel free to use additional paper.

The world is telling us to get real or get into reality, (such as, everybody is doing it, or, It won't hurt you or it's only beer), but this is not reality— Jesus said. In John 14:6:

_____

_____

_____

When Jesus said He was the truth He was telling us that He is REALITY. If we want to live in reality and not in virtual reality as the world wants to live, we will walk with Jesus and not with the world

Many people will simply tell the alcoholic/drug addict to just put down the alcohol and/or drugs. However, many of them can't! It's like telling the new born Christian to just pick up the Bible and everything will be okay. And of course, everything won't be okay. There is more that is needed.

My heart is to minister to the alcoholic and/or drug addict. Not just throw the "BOOK" at them, but to be a light in the darkness, accepting of the person—not the sin—as a human being created in the image of God.

The answer is a personal relationship with Jesus. Let's lift up the Lord, let us minister as we were ministered to and accepted by God.

(Romans 5:6): _____

_____

_____

God did not ask us to get better before we came to Him. He cleaned us up after coming to Him. We are new creations because of Him. It is because of Him that the old has passed away, not because of what you or I do.

(Romans 10:9-10): _____

_____

_____

_____

_____

_____

(Philippians 2:13): _____

_____

_____

(Acts 17:16-33)

16 While Paul was waiting for them in Athens, he was greatly distressed to see that the city was full of idols.
17 So he reasoned in the synagogue with the Jews and the God-fearing Greeks, as well as in the marketplace day by day with those who happened to be there.
18 A group of Epicurean and Stoic philosophers began to dispute with him. Some of them asked, "What is this babbler trying to say?" Others remarked, "He seems to be advocating foreign gods." They said this because Paul was preaching the good news about Jesus and the resurrection.
19 Then they took him and brought him to a meeting of the Areopagus, where they said to him, "May we know what this new teaching is that you are presenting?
20 You are bringing some strange ideas to our ears, and we want to know what they mean."
21 (All the Athenians and the foreigners who lived there spent their time doing nothing but talking about and listening to the latest ideas.)
22 Paul then stood up in the meeting of the Areopagus and said: "Men of Athens! I see that in every way you are very religious.

23 For as I walked around and looked carefully at your objects of worship, I even found an altar with this inscription: TO AN UNKNOWN GOD. Now what you worship as something unknown I am going to proclaim to you.

24 "The God who made the world and everything in it is the Lord of heaven and earth and does not live in temples built by hands.

25 And he is not served by human hands, as if he needed anything, because he himself gives all men life and breath and everything else.

26 From one man he made every nation of men, that they should inhabit the whole earth; and he determined the times set for them and the exact places where they should live.

27 God did this so that men would seek him and perhaps reach out for him and find him, though he is not far from each one of us.

28 'For in him we live and move and have our being.' As some of your own poets have said, 'We are his offspring.'

29 "Therefore since we are God's offspring, we should not think that the divine being is like gold or silver or stone—an image made by man's design and skill.

30 In the past God overlooked such ignorance, but now he commands all people everywhere to repent.

31 For he has set a day when he will judge the world with justice by the man he has appointed. He has given proof of this to all men by raising him from the dead."

32 When they heard about the resurrection of the dead, some of them sneered, but others said, "We want to hear you again on this subject."

33 At that, Paul left the Council.

o o o

In the passage above, Paul addresses the Jews and God-fearing Greeks in Athens concerning an idol they have erected to an unknown god.

This message is for us today. God is not a doorknob. He's not whatever you want him to be. He's not known through any other deity or prophet, or anyone, or anything else. God is who He said He is, the great "I AM"; King of Kings and Lord of Lords and only through a relationship with Jesus Christ is God understood as the Great "I Am."

Remember Jesus went among sinners to minister, not to beat them up. The Word of God tells us, "It was the sick who need a physician, not those who are well." Let us go and bring the Good News of the healing power of Christ and deliverance from substance dependence and acts of our sinful nature.

Chapter 2
Laying a Foundation

Before we start the steps out of bondage and begin the climb up the Victory Ladder, let's take a look at how we got caught in the snare of God's enemy.

In the second chapter of Genesis we see that after God created Adam and Eve, He placed them in the Garden. This is where they would have fellowship with God. They were given everything they would need to live and prosper, nothing was lacking. This is the place where man walked with God the Father in the cool of the day. Imagine what that was like. Adam and Eve were no strangers to the presence of God.

I imagine they talked about how the day went. Adam may have discussed the naming of the living creatures. He may have asked, "Lord, what do you think about the ones over there, the ones with the long neck and the funny spots? Look how they eat from the tops of the trees." "I see them Adam, aren't they wonderful creatures?" "Yes Lord, the giraffe is surely a creature to behold."

It is here, in the garden, that man was given the opportunity of a life-time. God gave them the opportunity to make a choice.

(Genesis 2:15-17): _____

_____

_____

_____

Until this time man did not have to choose to follow God or to disobey Him. Man had not had anything to disobey. Now, man had to make a choice. He had something to choose from. He could obey God and not eat from the Tree of Knowledge of Good and Evil, or disobey God, and eat from the tree and die.

Many wrongly believe that what God was saying to Adam, was that there are many trees in the garden and two trees that are placed in the middle of the garden—the Tree of Life and the Tree of the Knowledge of Good and Evil. Now you cannot eat from one of them, and that one is The Tree of the Knowledge of Good and Evil. However, if we look closely in verse 16 of chapter 2, what God said was that man could eat from *any* tree in the garden.

That means all the trees including The Tree of the Knowledge of Good and Evil. Yes, man could eat of that tree, if he chose to do so. But God also said in Genesis (2:17):

> [17] "you must not eat from the tree of the knowledge of good and evil, for when you eat of it you will surely die."

The emphasis in verse 17 is on the consequence of man's decision (cognitive) and action (behaviors). In fact, to eat of The Tree of the Knowledge of Good and Evil would be in disobedience to God. Adam and Eve would then experience what it means to be out of fellowship with God, they would know spiritual death. They would have lifted themselves up as equal to God.

The problem was not that they didn't know what they were to do or were not supposed to do. It was that Adam and Eve chose to act as God. Look very carefully at what is happening here. In Genesis (3:1) we see Satan speak falsely to Eve about what God had said. He questions Eve:

> [1] Now the serpent was more crafty than any of the wild animals the LORD God had made. He said to the woman, "Did God really say, 'You must not eat from any tree in the garden'?"

We know that this is not what God said because of verse 16 of Genesis 2. God said they could, eat from any tree. And then look what Eve says in Genesis (3:2-3):

> [2] The woman said to the serpent, "We may eat fruit from the trees in the garden,
> [3] but God did say, 'You must not eat fruit from the tree that is in the middle of the garden, and you must not touch it, or you will die.'"

The important thing about this statement is that Eve is wrong about what God said. She says that God said not to eat from the tree in the middle of the garden. Now how many trees were in the middle? Was there only one tree? No, there were two, The Tree of Life and The Tree of the Knowledge of Good and Evil. What happened here? Did she forget about the tree of life? Could she not see that there were two trees in the middle of the garden? What we see happening is that Eve was being deceived.

The definition of deceit involves falsehood or the deliberate concealment or misrepresentation of truth with the intent to lead another into error, or to disadvantage. Satan deliberately conceals the truth from Eve. He twists the Word of God. He lies. He deceives Eve.

This means that she was made to believe what is not true; misled, fooled by false promises. In Genesis (3:13b), we hear it from Eve:

_____

_____

The Hebrew word *naw-shaw* is used which means, *to lead astray mentally or to delude.* To the Corinthian church regarding false prophets Paul described it this way in 2 Corinthians (11:3):

_____

_____

_____

_____

From the beginning Satan does everything he can to lead us away from God. He attempts to hide the truth from us. He gets us to take our eyes off of Christ. But, Jesus said, in John (12:32):

_____

_____

_____

And in John (14:7): _____

_____

_____

And also in John (8:51): _____

_____

_____

Alleluia, the promises of God are yes and amen, and we can hold on to the promises, because they are true. God made them. Amen!

But what does Satan promise Eve? He promises her (Genesis 3:4):

⁴"You will not surely die," the serpent said to the woman.

The father of lies weaves his deception. He offers an alternative, just as he does so many times today. Satan offers Eve a lie woven in a bit of truth. He says to her (Genesis 3:5):

⁵*"For God knows that when you eat of it your eyes will be opened, and you will be like God, knowing good and evil."*

Satan plants into Eve's mind the idea that she will be like God, having the knowledge of what is right and wrong. This is something that Adam and Eve did not know about yet. They had not done anything to be ashamed of yet. They did not know what it was like to disobey. But the trap had been set. Let's look at the next verse.

In verse 6, we are told that Eve now saw that the fruit of the tree was good for food and pleasing to the eye (and this is what God said in Genesis chapter 2 verse 9), but Eve sees something else—she sees that it is also desirable for gaining wisdom. What she sees is that the fruit will provide her and Adam the ability to be the expert, or "God." The word used here is *saw-kal* and means; *to be, to make or act.* It includes the idea of being skilled or expert. In the context of what is happening at this time, we can understand that the deception of Satan was to get Adam and Eve to believe that they could be equal with God. They could have the ability to decide what is right or wrong, apart from of obedience to God's Word.

We must understand that seeking wisdom apart from God is not good; it is not what God intended for us. We are not to exalt ourselves to the place of equality with God and choose what is right and wrong. No, it is in obedience to the Word of God from which we are to choose right from wrong.

What is right and wrong is set forth by God in his Word. It is God's Word that is true and holy. It is what brings the promises of God to completion. Isn't that the same for us? Don't we face the same situation in our lives? If we want, we can choose to sin and disobey God, or choose to be obedient.

Look what Paul said (1 Corinthians 6:12): _____

And (1 Corinthians 10:23): _____

We have to make the same choice not to let anything have mastery over us or lead us away from God. We know the enemy is positioned ready to devour God's children. We know that sin is crouching at the door, ready to master us. But we are to be masters over sin. And with the help of the Holy Spirit and the wisdom of God we can stand firm in obedience to God. Amen!

The Problem of Addiction

Addiction is a Spiritual, Cognitive, and Behavioral disease which manifests as Alcoholism, Drug Dependence, and other behavioral addictions (i.e. sex, food, and gambling). The root of alcohol or substance dependence is Spiritual. Let's look at some of the biblical ideas.

A. (I Corinthians 6:9-10): _____

_____

_____

_____

_____

B. (Galatians 5:19-21): _____

_____

_____

_____

_____

_____

Notice that 1 Corinthians addresses the person, that is, both the Spiritual (our relationship to God) and Cognitive (our thoughts and decisions) aspects of the act. It identifies the drunkard, the person who drinks to excess. It also speaks of the mind when it tells us not to be deceived.

The passage in Galatians speaks to the behavior of the person, by addressing the act of drunkenness. Drunkenness is an act of our sinful nature. Thus, it is sin! It does not say drinking is a sin. However, drinking to intoxication is sin, and sin has a purpose: It kills, steals, or destroys us; and is obligated to do so. A wage is an obligation. Sin must master us and has an obligation to kill us.

(Romans 6:23): _____
_____
_____

(Romans 4:4): _____
_____
_____

We make the choice; the addict (referring to all addictions) makes a choice in the beginning. We all start drinking or using (whatever our drug of choice is), for the same reason—the effect. It's always for the effect; to be happy, to deal with pain, to relax, to fit in, to forget, to enjoy life, etc. The thing we choose, whether alcohol, drugs, lust, gambling, food, or pornography, becomes the drug of choice, because it does what the other drugs don't do.

In all of this we choose to play God, wanting to decide what is right or wrong instead of choosing right from wrong based on the Word of God. In other words, many of us choose to write our own story. As we persist in writing our own story, and persist in acts of our sinful nature, we become a slave, in bondage, addicted to the substance or process.

What we identify as alcoholism, drug addictions, sex addiction, food addictions, compulsive gambling, or any other addiction is the manifestation of the Spiritual bondage. This is the result of the power of sin, as it carries out its obligation to kill, steal, or destroy us.

Chapter 3
God Provides the Solution: Faith—Step 1

Just as the problem is spiritual, cognitive, and behavioral, the solution is as well; Jeremiah (17:10) tells us,

> ¹⁰ *"I the LORD search the heart and examine the mind, to reward a man according to his conduct, according to what his deeds deserve."*

Since the fall of man in the garden, we have been fighting the idea that we are not God. It's a battle we fight today. It's the battle we fight in our relationships, our addictions, illnesses, and our everyday walk with God. We don't like the way things are, how we feel, or who we are. We want the world to be the way we want it to be. When it's not, we choose to do what we think is necessary to make it the way we want. We act as if we are God and act according to what we believe is right for us. We do not seek God's way for us. We do not ask God, "what should I do?"

(Colossians 1:21): _____

_____

_____

In this Scripture, we find all the elements of disobedience to God, and the foundation of addiction. Our alienation from God addresses the spiritual aspect. The fact we are enemies of God in our minds speaks to the cognitive thought processes. Then, we see the behavioral part: in the evil things we do.

The climb to victory begins when we get honest, and understand that we have sinned and are in need of Gods' saving grace.

(Romans 3:10-12): _____

_____

_____

We are the problem, not other people, places, or things. It is us—you and me. We have been playing God. We want to live life the way we want, not the way God wants. We do not choose to live out the story God has written. We want to be the author of our own story. However, we must acknowledge that God, Who is the Author and Finisher of our Faith, is also the main character in the story. Romans (10:8-11) relates:

> [8] But what does it say? "The word is near you; it is in your mouth and in your heart," that is, the word of faith we are proclaiming: [9] That if you confess with your mouth, "Jesus is Lord," and believe in your heart that God raised him from the dead, you will be saved. [10] For it is with your heart that you believe and are justified, and it is with your mouth that you confess and are saved.
> [11] As the Scripture says, "Anyone who trusts in him will never be put to shame."

When we give our heart to the Lord, and are born again, and accept Jesus as Lord and Savior, we are given a measure of faith that enables us to begin the climb up the ladder—out of unfaithfulness (disloyalty), to victory.

First, however, we must understand that faith is a gift from the Father.

(Romans 12:3): _____

_____

_____

This gift is the faith that saves us, and it was nothing we did to obtain it.

(Ephesians 2:8-9): _____

_____

_____

_____

_____

_____

And since we are the workmanship of God (Ephesians 2:10): _____

_____

_____

_____

_____ it is the gift of faith that enables us to do His will in our life. The Scripture tells us that Jesus is the Author and Finisher of our Faith.

(Hebrews 12:2): _____

_____

_____

_____

_____

There's a saying in recovery that sobriety is simple but not easy. I have asked this question many times in group: "Is sobriety simple?" I usually get the same immediate answer. "No." However, when you really think about it, it is simple—just don't do it. Just don't use drugs or drink alcohol, abuse food, watch pornography, or compulsively gamble. It's just that simple. But instead, the focus is usually on the thought, "but just stopping is not always the easy part." God has provided the solution to the problem. He knows it isn't easy.

In fact, in John (15:5) He says, ⁵ "I am the vine; you are the branches. If a man remains in me and I in him, he will bear much fruit; apart from me you can do nothing."

However, (Philippians 4:13): _____

_____

_____

That means we can recover from our addictions.

God knows it is a tough hill to climb. He understands that what He asks of us we cannot accomplish. Because He loves us and wants us to succeed, He takes the first step for us. He gives us a measure of faith. But it doesn't end there. He makes sure we are able to do what he asks of us. Here's how He does it.

God tells us what He wants us to do. Then, He tells us how to do it, and then He provides us with the ability to do it. For example:

> ³⁷Jesus replied: "'Love the Lord your God **(what)** with all your heart and with all your soul and with all your mind.' **(how)** ³⁸ This is the first and greatest commandment. ³⁹ And the second is like it: 'Love your neighbor **(what)** as yourself.'**(how)** ⁴⁰ All the Law and the Prophets hang on these two commandments." (Matthew 22:37-40)

> ²⁷ "But I tell you who hear me: Love your enemies do good to those who hate you, **(what)**, ²⁸ bless those who curse you, pray for those who mistreat you. **(how)** (Luke 6:27-28)

> ²⁵ Husbands, love your wives **(what)**, just as Christ loved the church and gave himself up for her. **(how)** (Ephesians 5:25)

> ³⁴ "A new command I give you: Love one another **(what)**. As I have loved you **(how)**, so you must love one another. (John 13:34)

Then, He provides the ability to do it. We receive the Holy Spirit, the power to do what God has commanded of us.

> *⁸ But you will receive power when the Holy Spirit comes on you; and you will be my witnesses in Jerusalem, and in all Judea and Samaria, and to the ends of the earth. (Acts 1:8)*

By the power of the Holy Spirit, we are able to enter and stay sober. Why? Because, *¹³ "I can do everything through him who gives me strength."* (Philippians 4:13)

God took the first step, as He always does. The first step for *us* is to put our faith in the one who is faithful. God the Father, through His Son Jesus Christ and the power of the Holy Spirit, has given us the ability to climb up the Victory Ladder, out of bondage, to walk in Love.

(2 Peter 1:1-4): _____

_____

_____

_____

_____

_____

_____

_____

_____

_____

_____

_____

What is faith? Hebrews (11:1) tells us: _____

_____

_____

In everyday life we exercise faith. Think about it. When you go into a room and sit in a chair you are exercising faith the moment you sit in it. As you enter, you believe that the chair will support you. It has happened so many times before that you are not even questioning if it will this time or not. You approach the chair and sit down. This is the act of faith. Faith is the action you take based on what you believe or hope for. Because the chair has been faithful, in fact because other chairs have been faithful, you have developed a basic trust in chairs. Until a chair proves to be unfaithful, you will act in faith each time you choose to sit in a chair.

God has taken care of the first step in providing us with the measure of faith needed to climb the Victory Ladder out of the bondage of our sinful desires. Our responsibility is to exercise that faith. This becomes easier as we get honest with ourselves, others, and God; and begin to trust Him, ourselves, and others.

Later, as we climb the Victory Ladder we will examine in greater detail the truth about who God is. Now, however, we want to learn a bit about the faithfulness of God.

> [19] Now we know that whatever the law says, it says to those who are under the law, so that every mouth may be silenced and the whole world held accountable to God. [20] Therefore no one will be declared righteous in his sight by observing the law; rather, through the law we become conscious of sin.
>
> [21] But now a righteousness from God, apart from law, has been made known, to which the Law and the Prophets testify. [22] This righteousness from God comes through faith in Jesus Christ to all who believe. There is no difference, [23] for all have sinned and fall short of the glory of God, [24] and are justified freely by his grace through the redemption that came by Christ Jesus.
>
> [25] God presented him as a sacrifice of atonement, through faith in his blood. He did this to demonstrate his justice, because in his forbearance he had left the sins committed beforehand unpunished— [26] he did it to demonstrate his justice at the present time, so as to be just and the one who justifies those who have faith in Jesus. [27] Where, then, is boasting? It is excluded. On what principle? On that of observing the law? No, but on that of faith.

> ²⁸ For we maintain that a man is justified by faith apart from observing the law. ²⁹ Is God the God of Jews only? Is he not the God of Gentiles too? Yes, of Gentiles too, ³⁰ since there is only one God, who will justify the circumcised by faith and the uncircumcised through that same faith. ³¹ Do we, then, nullify the law by this faith? Not at all! Rather, we uphold the law. (Romans 3:19-3)

We see here, that as born again believers, we are no longer under the law. We have been set free from the law. We do not follow the commandments of God as under the obligation of a law, but our obedience to Gods' laws is through the exercise of our faith, thus, we have God's righteousness and are made righteous.

Think about it in practical terms. Each State sets speed limit laws. As I drive down the road exceeding the posted speed limit, I see a patrol car and know I have just been caught transgressing the law. Under that law I must obey its limitations or suffer the negative consequences of breaking the law. However, when I act in faith concerning the speed limit laws, I obey them even if there is no patrol car. I stay within the limits because it's the right thing to do. The exercise of my faith is demonstrated in abiding by the speed limits, and it does not do away with the law, it upholds the law.

This is the same in our struggles with addictions. The laws of alcoholism, drug addiction and other bondages seem impossible to obey. However, trusting in God and putting our faith in Him to strengthen us to break free from those bondages, satisfies the law.

As we develop this strength instead of trying to prove how strong we are, He promises to be faithful and keep us sober.

(1 Corinthians 1:8-9): _____

_____

_____

_____

_____

_____

_____

Even in our moment to moment struggles (relapses), He remains faithful:

> ¹³ if we are faithless, he will remain faithful, for he cannot disown himself. (2 Timothy 2:13)

You see, as believers we have been bought with a price. We belong to God the Father, and He can't and won't turn His back on His children. What an encouragement. The Lord God almighty is in our corner. How can we ever be defeated? We cannot!

(Matthew 7:13-14): _____

_____

_____

_____

_____

_____

The first exercise (Road of Life-facing page) for this step is a divided road. On the left side, the wide road, you are to draw pictures of real life situations that have brought you to your present situation. This is the road you chose. The other side is the narrow way. This is the, "What could have been side." Follow the road signs along the way. You will share this in group.

Road of Life

1. Begin in the square box labeled "Present" by drawing something that represents where you are in your life now (entered program) with God.
2. Then complete the "Real Life Happenings" side of the road by starting at the "1 year ago" space. In that space, draw an important event that happened then that has played a role in leading you to the present.
3. In the "5 years ago" space draw an important event (from 5 years ago) that helped lead you to the 1 year ago event and the present.
4. Do the same as above in the "10 years ago" space.
5. Do the same in the "20 years ago" space.
6. Now, move to the "What Could Have Been" side and look at the event you drew in the 1 year space. Draw something you could have done (what could have been if you had recognized God was in your life) to change what happened in your life one year ago.
7. Now move to the 5 year space and do the same.
8. Do the same in the 10 year space.
9. Do the same in the 20 year space.

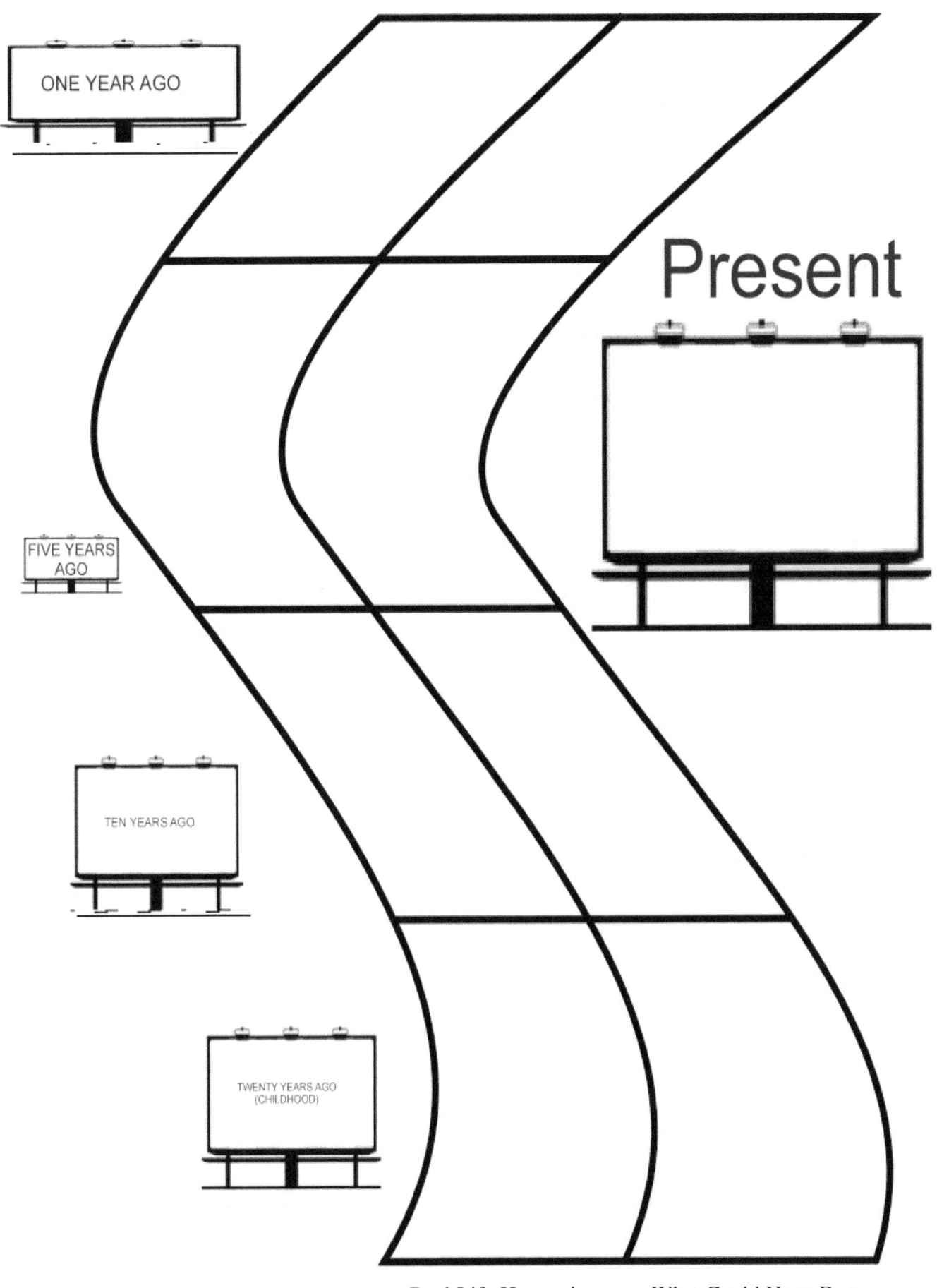

My Life Story

Next you will write a "Life Story" as it happened. This should include: substance use (include amounts and types of drugs or alcohol), criminal activity, relationships (God, parents, siblings, friends, etc.). It should also include your feelings toward these relationships and the times, in looking back, you can see where God was in your life, though, at the time you did not recognize Him. We want to get an understanding of the story you have written for yourself. Add as many additional pages as necessary.

_____
_____
_____
_____
_____
_____
_____
_____
_____
_____
_____
_____
_____
_____
_____

Chapter 4
Trust & Change—Step 1

The second part of Step One, on the path toward victory, is trust. We begin by putting our trust in God who has always been faithful. Trust is having faith in someone or something. We start with trusting the faithfulness of God and then extend faith and trust in others.

This part of the first step (faith) is all about trusting God with our life. Not just parts of it, but in every aspect of it, especially in our recovery from addiction.

(Proverbs 3:5-6): _____

_____

_____

We've looked at the faithfulness of God. We have considered what faith is. Now we must put that faith into action and trust God. Our faith must become "living faith."

> [20] He replied, "Because you have so little faith. I tell you the truth, if you have faith as small as a mustard seed, you can say to this mountain, 'Move from here to there' and it will move. Nothing will be impossible for you. (Matthew 17:20)

The focus is not on size, for God honors even a small faith. It is the idea that as the mustard seed is nurtured and grows, so does our faith. Faith needs to be exercised and active, to ensure that it grows and becomes stronger, so that we may do great things, such as stay clean and sober.

Many people, places and things have let us down. We have decided not to trust others, sometimes even ourselves, and yes, especially God. But there is One: One Who can be trusted, Who does not let us down, Who will not leave us, and does not lie to us. That One is God.

> ¹⁹ God is not a man, that he should lie, nor a son of man, that he should change his mind. Does he speak and then not act? Does he promise and not fulfill? (Numbers 23:19)

And, He says (Hebrews 13:5b), "Never will I leave you; never will I forsake you." Also in Deuteronomy (31:6) ⁶ Be strong and courageous. Do not be afraid or terrified because of them, for the LORD your God goes with you; he will never leave you nor forsake you."

That narrow road you laid out in the previous exercise was one scenario of what could have been. It may or may not have been the story God is actually writing for you, but we do know that it is an alternative to the story you have been writing for yourself. Now, we begin to trust God and live in His story. We live according to how He says to live. It is time to live Gods' way, by faith walking in the Spirit.

(Romans 8:12-16): _____

_____

_____

_____

_____

_____

_____

_____

Walking in the Spirit is a path we want to begin taking. This is the path that is God's will for our life. When we trust in Him, seek His direction, acknowledge Him in all of our affairs, He says that He will direct our path. That narrow road that leads to victory, "The Victory Ladder," becomes climbable and we are able to walk in the grace of God. We walk in Love.

In this step, things must begin to change. In recovery it is said, we must change our playgrounds, playmates, and playthings. While this is true, there is something else we must understand. We must also understand that some things we can change, and some things only God can change.

Everything changes! Talk with a person for a few minutes and he or she will probably tell you about something they want to change, or someone who needs to change. If the weather is cold, we complain and want it to be warmer. In the summer we want the weather to change so it will be cooler. When it rains, we want the sun to shine. When it's dry out, someone is praying for rain. In relationships we pray or wish, if only "he" or "she" would change then everything would be better. In our jobs we wish, "if only I had a different boss or better hours or didn't have to work at all." If, If, If. If only this and if only that. Lord, please change my world so I can be happy.

In the Word of God we see that God changed the name of a person to reflect a change in purpose or character. In Genesis (17: 5) Abram (exalted father) became Abraham (father of many). In verse 15 of that same chapter, Abraham is to no longer call his wife Sarai. She will be called Sarah, blessed with a son and be the mother of many nations and even kings shall come from her.

We also read of Saul, who becomes the apostle to the Gentles and is called Paul in Acts (13:9). In John (15:15) Jesus says we are now called friends:

> [15] I no longer call you servants, because a servant does not know his master's business. Instead, I have called you friends, for everything that I learned from my Father I have made known to you. (John 15:15)

It seems that change is one thing we can count on. It is a constant. I am sure you've heard the saying, "the one thing you can count on is change" or "the only permanent thing is change."

Let's look at change, and what God's Word says about change. We are going to look at two very important truths of God's Word in relationship to what He does change, and that which He does not change. Let's start with the unchangeable or unchanging.

We live in a world that seems to be ever changing. We are told that the one constant is "change." However, let's set the record straight. There is one who does not change, who is truly constant, and who remains the same. No matter what is going on in the world, or happening in your life, Jehovah, the Lord Almighty remains the same.

The Word of God tells us, our heavenly Father, the one and only true God, the creator of this changing world does not change. Look at Malachi (3:6): [6] "I the LORD do not change. So you, O descendants of Jacob, are not destroyed..."

Have you ever truly considered what that tells you? Do you realize what that means for us in an ever-changing world? Think about it for a moment!

1. Each day we hear that the Stock Market is going up or down–causing concern for our financial stability.

2. On any given day we may get a report that some study has shown 'this" or 'that" will kill us. Then, a month or years later, a new study says "maybe not"— causing confusion about our well-being.

3. Reports continually change regarding health issues. What is healthy for us, what is not? Who do we listen to?

4. This includes; I change. I change my thinking and my behaviors. At times it's not always for the better.

Can you sense the uncertainty in all this change? When it's listened to, it creates fear. As believers, we do not have to listen. We need to understand, we have a heavenly Father who tells us, don't worry about a thing. In Psalm (103:3) He says:

_____

_____

_____

He tells us (Philippians 4:19): _____

_____

Now, can you hear the Holy Spirit reminding you of the promises of God? That the Father has not changed and He never will. It's also important that we understand that God also does not change His mind. 1 Samuel (15:29) tells us:

_____

_____

_____

And in Psalm (110:4) we see that: _____

_____

In John (14:6), [6] Jesus answered, "I am the way and the truth and the life. No one comes to the Father except through me." It's plain and simple, The Lord does not change. He did it before and He'll do it again. Amen!

We need to say "thank You Lord, for being that one constant in the world and my life." He's the One we can count on to be there, the one that remains the same. He will *always* remain the same. He "is the same yesterday and today and forever." (Hebrews 13:8)

Can we truly begin to grasp the powerful truth about Our Lord and Savior? He does not change in a constantly changing world. This is a truth we must get deep within our hearts. This truth must be our foundation if we are to build on the promises of God. Hang on to this and remind yourselves daily. Remember, we walk by faith and not by sight.

Now, let's look at something that may shock some of you. It may seem strange to others. And some may think, "what have I got myself into? What is this guy going to say now?" Well, I ask that you follow along closely in your Bible and study the Scripture, and you will see these truths. So here we go.

There is a very important truth we need to be aware of concerning what changes God does make. I am not talking about God changing. I am talking about the changes God makes in us.

What we need to see, is that there are only two things about us that God has said that He is going to change for us. Just two: not three, not four, not five, not ten, or whatever number you say. If fact, He changes these two things because we are incapable of changing them.

The first thing God tells us He will change happens when we became born-again—when we come to know Jesus Christ as Lord and Savior. When we are in Christ, He makes a change in us that we are not able to do ourselves. **We are made a new creation.**

Look at 2 Corinthians (5:17): _____

_____

_____

_____

When we are made a new creation, God changes our sinful nature. At one time we were all sinners, we all fall short of God's glory, (Romans 3:23): **"for all have sinned and fall short of the glory of God."** In Romans (8:7) "the sinful mind is hostile to God. It does not submit to God's law, nor can it do so." In Romans (7:4-5):

> [4] So, my brothers, you also died to the law through the body of Christ, that you might belong to another, to him who was raised from the dead, in order that we might bear fruit to God. [5] For when we were controlled by the sinful nature, the sinful passions aroused by the law were at work in our bodies, so that we bore fruit for death.

But now, through the work of Christ on the cross we are made new. [24] *"Those who belong to Christ Jesus have crucified the sinful nature with its passions and desires."* (Galatians 5:24). The old has become new. Once I was a slave to sin, but now in Christ I have been set free, no longer a slave to sin but a slave to righteousness.

Look at (Romans 6:16-18): _____

_____

_____

_____

_____

_____

We have been set free to do that which is right. Now, through obedience to God's Word, we can choose to do what is right. Because God has changed in us what we could not change in ourselves. "Thank You Lord!"

The second thing that God says He is going to change that we are incapable of changing, is **our complete appearance**. I am not talking about a new hair style or a makeover like some TV star. I'm talking about **a complete transformation** of who we are.

(1 Corinthians 15:51-52): _____

_____

_____

_____

_____

_____

We won't be the same; the perishable will become imperishable, mortal to immortal. We will be changed. We will no longer be as we are now, but will be as He is:

> ² Dear friends, now we are children of God, and what we will be has not yet been made known. But we know that when he appears, we shall be like him, for we shall see him as he is. (1 John 3:2)

These are the two changes that God has said He will make, because we are unable to make these changes ourselves. These changes are impossible without God. God takes care of the first one when we turn our life over to Him and are born-again, and He takes care of the second when the last trumpet is sounded. However, as exciting as that is, the point for us to understand is this:

God has made the changes He had to make, so that we can make changes in our life so that we are to make changes in the world in which we live. And to make those changes, we must know who we are in Christ, or nothing changes. The responsibility to change is not in Gods' hands, it is in ours.

Look at the following Scriptures:

> ¹ Therefore, I urge you, brothers, in view of God's mercy, to offer your bodies as living sacrifices, holy and pleasing to God—this is your spiritual act of worship.
> ² Do not conform any longer to the pattern of this world, but be transformed by the renewing of your mind. Then you will be able to test and approve what God's will is—his good, pleasing and perfect will. (Romans 12:1-2)

> ²⁵ Thanks be to God—through Jesus Christ our Lord! So then, I myself in my mind am a slave to God's law, but in the sinful nature a slave to the law of sin. (Romans 7:25)

> ⁵ Those who live according to the sinful nature have their minds set on what that nature desires; but those who live in accordance with the Spirit have their minds set on what the Spirit desires. (Romans 8:5)
>
> ⁷ the sinful mind is hostile to God. It does not submit to God's law, nor can it do so. ⁸ Those controlled by the sinful nature cannot please God. ⁹ You, however, are controlled not by the sinful nature but by the Spirit, if the Spirit of God lives in you. And if anyone does not have the Spirit of Christ, he does not belong to Christ. ¹⁰ But if Christ is in you, your body is dead because of sin, yet your spirit is alive because of righteousness. ¹¹ And if the Spirit of him who raised Jesus from the dead is living in you, he who raised Christ from the dead will also give life to your mortal bodies through his Spirit, who lives in you. ¹² Therefore, brothers, we have an obligation—but it is not to the sinful nature, to live according to it. (Romans 8:8-12)
>
> ¹⁶ "For who has known the mind of the Lord that he may instruct him?" But we have the mind of Christ. (1 Corinthians 2:16)

It is so important that we understand that it is not God who is going to change everything for us. He has already done what He needed to do, so we can live the way He wants us to live.

Are you willing to go through life not really knowing who you are in Christ? God has done His work. He has made us new creations in Christ. He will change us to be fully like Him in the twinkling of an eye. But it is up to us to grow in faith, renew our minds, and trust in Christ so we can walk in His ways. So when Jesus returns He will find us about the Father's business. And we will hear Him say as in Matthew (25:23):

_____

_____Amen!

Throughout the Scripture, God has told us what He wants us to do. He tells us how to do it and He gives us the power to do it. Our responsibility is to search the Word of God and learn who we are in Christ, which will enable us to make the changes God has left up to us. He put it like this (Galatians 5:13-25):

> [13] You, my brothers, were called to be free. But do not use your freedom to indulge the sinful nature; rather, serve one another in love. [14] The entire law is summed up in a single command: "Love your neighbor as yourself." [15] If you keep on biting and devouring each other, watch out or you will be destroyed by each other. [16] So I say, live by the Spirit, and you will not gratify the desires of the sinful nature. [17] For the sinful nature desires what is contrary to the Spirit, and the Spirit what is contrary to the sinful nature. They are in conflict with each other, so that you do not do what you want. [18] But if you are led by the Spirit, you are not under law. [19] The acts of the sinful nature are obvious: sexual immorality, impurity and debauchery; [20] idolatry and witchcraft; hatred, discord, jealousy, fits of rage, selfish ambition, dissensions, factions[21] and envy; drunkenness, orgies, and the like. I warn you, as I did before, that those who live like this will not inherit the kingdom of God. [22] But the fruit of the Spirit is love, joy, peace, patience, kindness, goodness, faithfulness, [23] gentleness and self-control. Against such things there is no law. [24] Those who belong to Christ Jesus have crucified the sinful nature with its passions and desires. [25] Since we live by the Spirit, let us keep in step with the Spirit. [26] Let us not become conceited, provoking and envying each other.

This is why we can trust God.

The exercises for this part of the first step (faith) include the Life Cross and Life Wheel (found on the next two pages). Both exercises are discussed in group. When these have been successfully shared in your group, you then finish this chapter and step in a verbal testimony in your group.

Life Cross

1. At the top of the cross, draw something that shows how you have tried to play God.
2. To the right of the cross, draw something that shows where you lost trust in another person.
3. To the left of the cross, draw something acknowledging you did something wrong.
4. At the lower end of the cross, draw something that shows how you have lost trust in God.
5. At the foot of the cross, write in one sentence your commitment to begin trusting that God can and will forgive you.

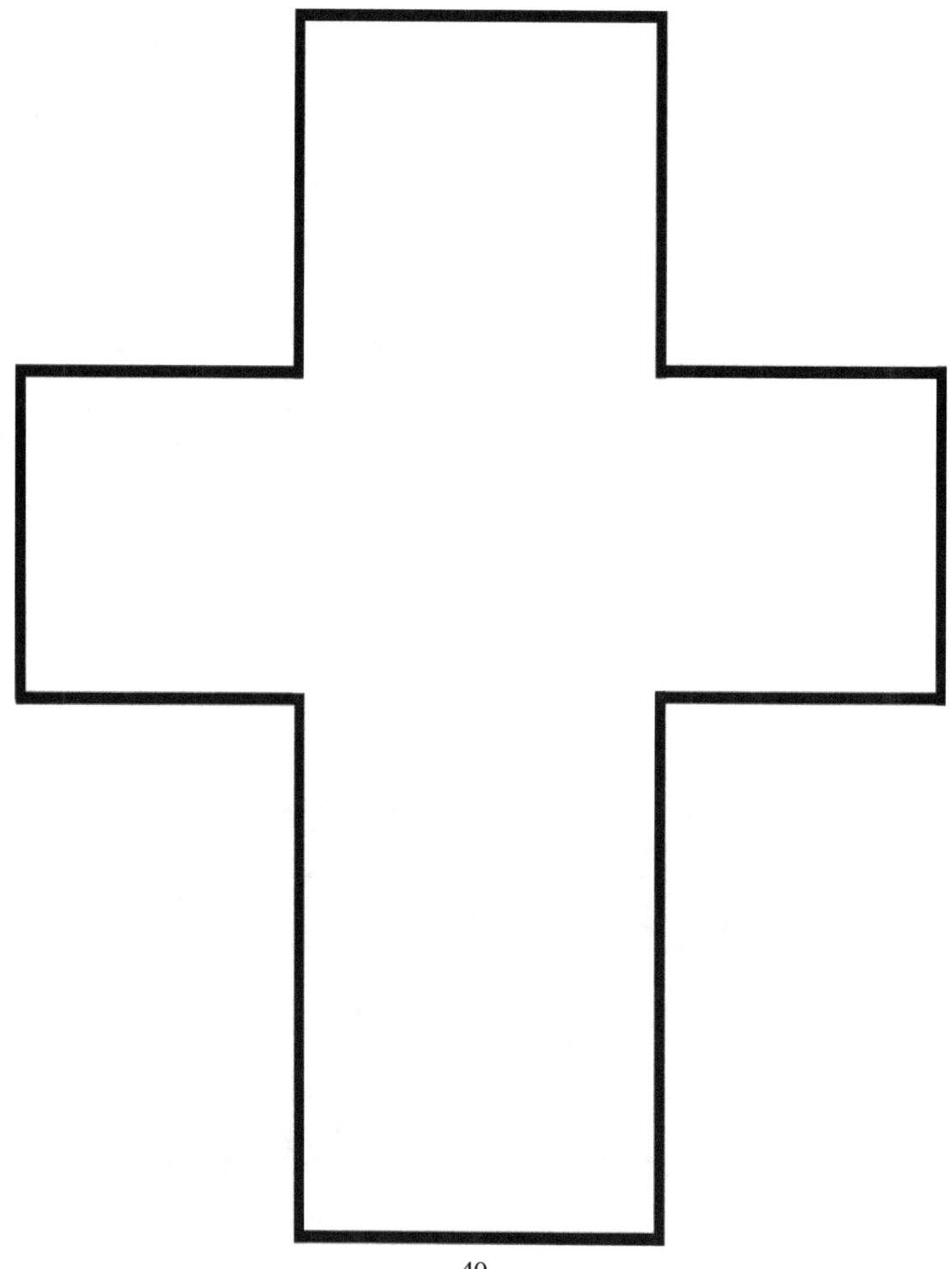

Life Wheel

1. Draw a picture that represents the biggest fear in your life currently.
2. Draw a picture that represents what it is that is holding you back from being all that God wants you to be.
3. Draw a picture of something that you believe is holding you back from truly trusting God.
4. Draw a picture of something that you have not done, but knew God wanted you to do.
5. Draw a picture of something that you have done, and you knew God was involved in it.
6. Draw a picture of something that you believe God is leading you to do.
7. Draw a picture of the most important person in your life, other than yourself.
8. Draw a picture of the things in life that you believe will lead you to experience the joy of the Lord.

In the center, draw a picture that represents your current relationship with God.

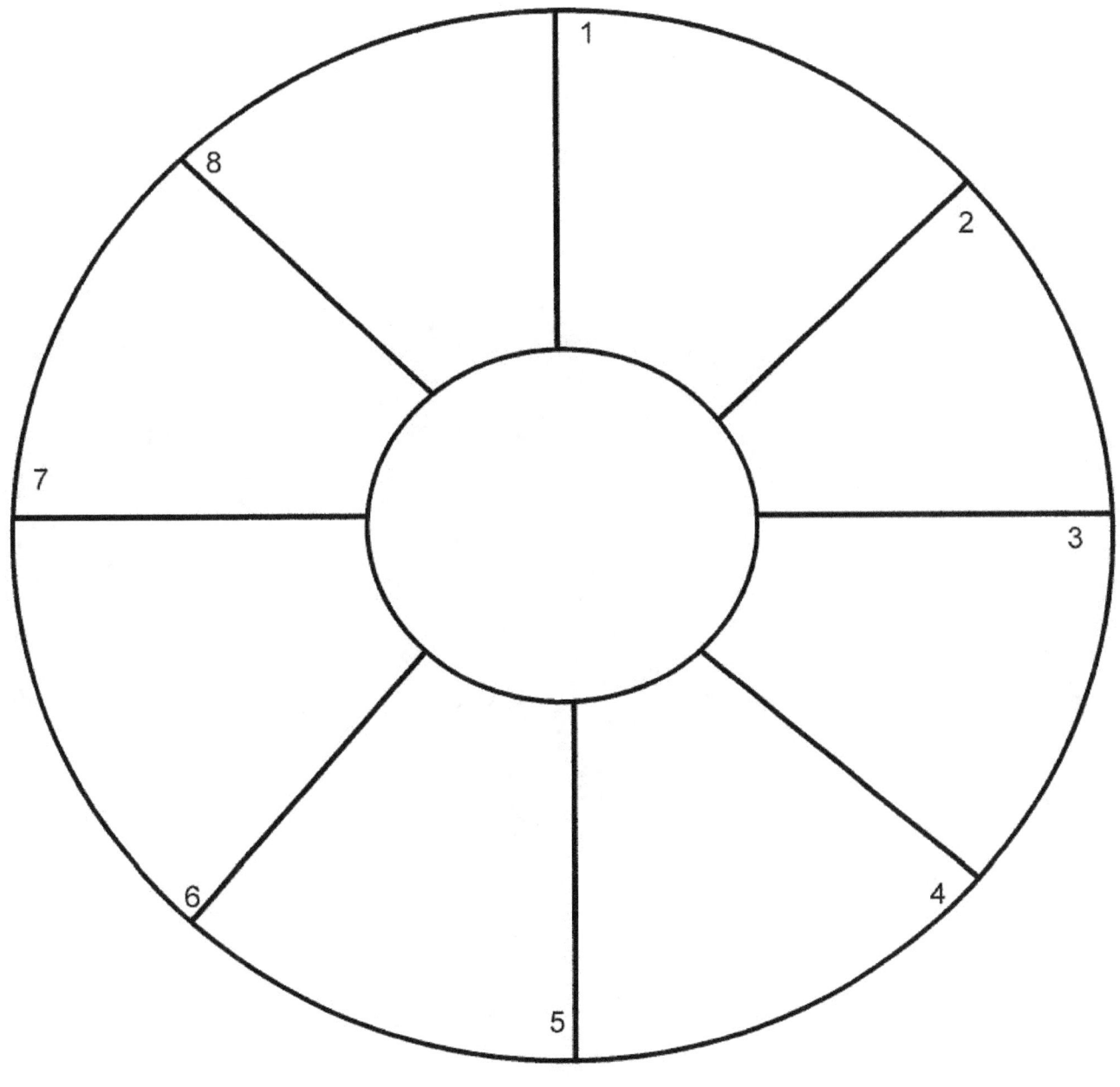

Step 1 Testimony

The last part of this step is a brief testimony covering the following:

1. That you trust God and will begin exercising faith in Him, and that you trust this program.

2. That you trust someone here.

3. A commitment to being honest with God, yourself, and others. When you fall back; you will trust God, yourself, and the program to restore you to a right standing with God.

4. That you are willing, and will begin to dialogue with God (i.e. pray, meditate and read the Bible).

Chapter 5
Goodness—Step 2

This step up the Victory Ladder is crucial. This is where the rubber meets the road. To continue to climb up the ladder and out of the bondage of your past, you must be willing to give up writing your own story and decide to walk in the story that God has written for you. You have to turn from being Gods' enemy and start being obedient to Him, by obeying His Word.

(2 Peter 1:3-4): _____

_____

_____

_____

_____

_____

God has provided everything we need for life. Not just enough to get by, but more than enough to be victorious in overcoming our addiction(s), or any of life's struggles: "No, in all these things we are more than conquerors through him who loved us." (Romans 8:37)

Shortly, you will be asked to consider, and make a life changing decision; one that will forever change who you are and your relationship with God. But for now, we are going to look at the goodness of God and what His Word says concerning adding goodness to your walk.

> ¹ I cry aloud to the LORD; I lift up my voice to the LORD for mercy. ² I pour out my complaint before him; before him I tell my trouble. ³ When my spirit grows faint within me, it is you who know my way. In the path where I walk men have hidden a snare for me. ⁴ Look to my right and see; no one is concerned for me. I have no refuge; no one cares for my life. ⁵ I cry to you, O LORD; I say, "You are my refuge, my portion in the land of the living." ⁶ Listen to my cry, for I am in desperate need; rescue me from those who pursue me, for they are too strong for me. ⁷ Set me free from my prison, that I may praise your name. Then the righteous will gather about me because of your goodness to me. (Psalms 142:1-7)

Doesn't this kind of sound like any given day in the life of addictions? At times, we all have felt weak, with no place to hide from the struggles of life, always running from the consequences of our choices. We feel like giving up, because we have no more strength to fight the cravings or obsessive thinking. We want out of the prison that our choices in life have put us in.

There is a way to escape your prison, a way to continue to move up the Victory Ladder. The first step, faith was God's goodness being shown in you by giving you a measure of faith to be all He desires for you. When you come to a place where you are ready to give up and let God be in charge, you experience the goodness of God. The goodness of God is expressed in two ways; His giving, and His forgiveness.

From the beginning, God has been giving and forgiving. God is always giving. He has given us life; "²⁸ 'For in him we live and move and have our being.' As some of your own poets have said, 'We are his offspring.'" (Acts 17:28)

He gives us everything that we need in life, (2 Peter 1:3): _____

_____

_____

_____

_____

He wants His children to be successful, "For I know the plans I have for you," declares the LORD, "plans to prosper you and not to harm you, plans to give you hope and a future." (Jeremiah 29:11) He gave so we could live life abundantly, in fact more abundantly, "The thief comes only to steal and kill and destroy; I have come that they may have life, and have it to the full." (John 10:10)

When we become obedient children, Jesus tells us that He will ask the Father to give us another Counselor that will be with us forever and teach us all truth.

(John 14:15-17): _____

_____

_____

_____

_____

_____

_____

This Counselor, the Holy Spirit, will not only give us the power and ability to remain clean and sober, but will also teach us all that Jesus wanted us to know so that we can be obedient children.

"What," You say. "Can I know everything that Jesus knows?" Well, 'YES, WE CAN.' Remember Jesus' words:

> ⁶ Jesus answered, "I am the way and the truth and the life. No one comes to the Father except through me. ⁷ If you really knew me, you would know my Father as well. From now on, you do know him and have seen him." (John 14:6-7)

Contrary to what others may say, there is only one way to the Father. That way is Jesus. Like it or not, that's just the way it is. It's what God says.

John the apostle tells us that Jesus did much more, and said much more than what is written in the Bible; "Jesus did many other things as well. If every one of them were written down, I suppose that even the whole world would not have room for the books that would be written." (John 21:25)

You get the idea. We don't have enough room for all that Jesus did and said. But since all of what Jesus did and said is important to us, God made sure that we had a way to know. So, He sent the Holy Spirit to teach us and remind us of the things Jesus did and said.

(John 14:25-26): _____

_____

_____

_____

_____

_____

_____

How much more giving and loving could God the Father be? He not only wrote it down for us and preserved what was written, but also wanted to make sure we had a way to know everything we would need to know to understand and be victorious in life. Now one thing we must understand is that when we ask the Holy Spirit to reveal the truth to us, we must remember that whatever is revealed will always line up with what is written in God's Word. Nothing can contradict the written Word of God.

Forgiveness

The second way that God's goodness is manifested is in His forgiveness. All of us have "blown it" in our lives. We have not been obedient to God, not respected ourselves, or others. We destroyed the trust that others had in us. We've let down our loved ones, and friends. We've missed out on precious time with our families. We have not achieved what we had dreamed about. And now, in our attempt to get clean and sober, we find that it isn't easy to forget, and at times almost impossible to forgive ourselves of all the things we have done—and not done.

But we must understand that God, in His goodness and love toward us, has provided a way for us to return to a right standing with Him.

"Praise the LORD, O my soul, and forget not all his benefits— ³ who forgives all your sins and heals all your diseases." (Psalms 103:2-3)

He says that in His forgiveness He will not even remember our sins; "For I will forgive their wickedness and will remember their sins no more." (Hebrews 8:12)

Understanding God's goodness, and walking in His forgiveness, enables us to do good things for others and be good to ourselves. We must now begin to exercise our faith and trust. Look at Romans (12:17-21) and then read James (2:14- 26).

Do not repay anyone evil for evil. Be careful to do what is right in the eyes of everybody.

> ¹⁸ If it is possible, as far as it depends on you, live at peace with everyone. ¹⁹ Do not take revenge, my friends, but leave room for God's wrath, for it is written: "It is mine to avenge; I will repay," says the Lord. ²⁰ On the contrary: "If your enemy is hungry, feed him; if he is thirsty, give him something to drink. In doing this, you will heap burning coals on his head." ²¹ Do not be overcome by evil, but overcome evil with good. (Romans 12:17-21)

(James 2:14-26): _____

_____

_____

_____

_____

_____

_____

_____

_____

_____

To exercise one's faith and trust, each of us must make a decision if we are to go any further. It is in knowing the goodness of God that we are enabled to trust in Him and turn to Him.

We now come to the pivotal point of your journey up the Victory Ladder. It is the only way anyone can reach the top. It is the only way you or I can understand the goodness of God or be of any good to others or ourselves. It is the place where we walk in love and in the fullness of Gods' grace. And, again, we see that God makes the first move. He gives us His Son: (John 3:16-17).

God sent His Son into the world to bring us back to Him. He provides the way for us to return to fellowship with Him; to walk with Him in the cool of the day once again. Just as He always does, He has done it just at the right time.

(Romans 5:6-8): _____

_____

_____

_____

_____

_____

_____

This step is about **acceptance**. Accepting the fact that you are unable to get or stay clean and sober on our own—you are the problem. Accepting that without God you are powerless to save yourself and in need of a Savior—a way back to God. To go on from here, you will need to make a life changing decision; one not to be taken lightly. It will forever change your life. Here are the steps you must take.

First, you must acknowledge you are a sinner and in need of a Savior. As it is written:

> "There is no one righteous, not even one; [11] there is no one who understands, no one who seeks God. [12] All have turned away, they have together become worthless; there is no one who does good, not even one." (Romans 3:10-12)

Second, you must exercise your faith and put your trust in God's gift to you by turning your life over to Jesus.

You do this through words. "The word is near you; it is in your mouth and in your heart" (Romans 10:8), that is, the word of faith we are proclaiming:

> ⁹ That if you confess with your mouth, "Jesus is Lord," and believe in your heart that God raised him from the dead, you will be saved.
> ¹⁰ For it is with your heart that you believe and are justified, and it is with your mouth that you confess and are saved. ¹¹ As the Scripture says, "Anyone who trusts in him will never be put to shame." ¹² For there is no difference between Jew and Gentile—the same Lord is Lord of all and richly blesses all who call on him, ¹³ for, "Everyone who calls on the name of the Lord will be saved." (Romans 10:8-11)

Third, you must acknowledge Him to others. "Whoever acknowledges me before men, I will also acknowledge him before my Father in heaven. ³³ But whoever disowns me before men, I will disown him before my Father in heaven." (Matthew 10:32-33)

Making this decision changes everything, not only you, but your entire world has changed. Imagine, you have with God's help, just changed the whole world. It is not the same as it was. The Bible says it this way, (2 Corinthians 5:17):

_____

_____

_____

If you, at some time in the past, made this decision and give your heart to the Lord, then this will be a time to rededicate your commitment to surrender to God. Having done this, you can now add goodness to your faith.

Through Jesus, therefore, let us continually offer to God a sacrifice of praise—the fruit of lips that confess his name.

> [16] And do not forget to do good and to share with others, for with such sacrifices God is pleased. (Hebrews 13:15-16)

There is one more exercise to complete in order to move to the next step. You must tell three people of the life changing decision you have made and bring proof that you have done so. A note from each person will be accepted or use the form below. Your experience will then be shared in group.

We, the undersigned, were told of the decision made by the owner of this book:

Person 1:_____ Date:_____
Comment:

Person 2:_____ Date:_____
Comment:

Person 3:_____ Date:_____
Comment:

Chapter 6
Knowledge—Step 3

In the last step you made a life changing decision. Whether you turned your life over to Jesus or chose to stay the way you were, the decision was one that set in motion the rest of your journey. If you chose to surrender to God and allow Him to rule your life, then you are ready to take the next step up the Victory Ladder.

The decision you made to turn your life over to Jesus was not just some good thing to do, or something that sounded good. It was a decision to follow Jesus—to let God direct your path. Part of that meant you chose to become His disciple. To be His disciple means you need to get to know who He is, and who God says you are. Remember, you are not anything God doesn't say you are.

This step is about becoming aware of who God is and who you are. Remember, when you gave your life to the Lord, you became a new creation. You are brand new. The old you is now gone, that person does not exist.

This step is to get you to start the process of being transformed by the renewing of your mind. It's time to know the truth about God, and who you are as His child. Jesus said, speaking to those who believed: *"If you hold to my teaching, you are really my disciples. Then you will know the truth, and the truth will set you free."* (John 8:31-32). This step is adding knowledge to goodness. Are you ready? Let's begin.

Adding knowledge to goodness begins with having a fear of God. "The fear of the LORD is the beginning of knowledge, but fools despise wisdom and discipline." (Proverbs 1:7). If you want to know how to stand firm and fearless, to defeat the enemy and all your fears, then develop a fear of the Lord.

Now, what do I mean by develop a **FEAR** of the Lord? I don't mean you should become afraid of Him as you might be afraid of someone who was about to do you harm or afraid of the dark. No, what the truth of God's Word tells us is that a fear of the Lord means that we are in "awe" of Him. Let's look at Psalm. (22:23); **"**You who fear the LORD, praise him! All you descendants of Jacob, honor him! Revere him, all you descendants of Israel!" and also, (Psalm 33:8-11):

> *⁸Let all the earth fear the LORD; let all the people of the world revere him. ⁹ For he spoke, and it came to be; he commanded, and it stood firm. ¹⁰ The LORD foils the plans of the nations; he thwarts the purposes of the peoples. ¹¹ But the plans of the LORD stand firm forever, the purposes of his heart through all generations.*

You see, to have a fear of the Lord is to be in awe of Him, to reverence, to be awestruck by His character and His Word. It means to be in awe of His mighty power and deeds, and reverence His righteous judgment—all His Wonder!

What a mighty, awesome God we serve! He is awesome in His power, majesty, splendor, holiness and glory. Amen! He's is the great I Am! He **IS** an awesome God; He reigns with wisdom and power, in Heaven and earth. He is beyond our ability to articulate; our God, what an awesome God!

A fear of God is not to run away from Him. No, to the contrary, it is to run to Him, to put your whole trust in Him. To fall before Him in awe and declare Him Lord of your life and your only strength, is to dispel all other fears. The fear of failure in recovery, the fear of success, the fear of rejection, the fear of embarrassment, the fear of disapproval, or the fear of being perceived as a failure—and even the fear of death. It matters not what your fear is.

When you have rightly developed a fear of the Lord, you will be able to cast down all other objects of fear. No other fear object can have power over you any longer. The fear of failure is cast down because (Philippians 4:13):

_____

_____

_____

> The fear of not being accepted is cast down because: "But God demonstrates his own love for us in this: While we were still sinners, Christ died for us." (Romans 5:8)
>
> The fear of rejection is cast down because: "Whoever acknowledges me before men, I will also acknowledge him before my Father in heaven." (Matthew 10:32)
>
> The fear of death is overcome because: "Where, O death, is your victory? Where, O death, is your sting?" (1 Corinthians 15:55)

What an awesome God, that even the fear and power of the grave has been removed! All your fears can be cast down, thrown to the side of the road if you will. When you bring yourself before your Heavenly Father, and in awesome wonder, trust and obey, bow in humble adoration to the Great I AM, and develop a fear of the Lord, you will stand firm. You will be able to stand as Paul did and declare (Romans 1:16):

_____

_____

_____

_____

When we have the truth of whom God is and who we are, we never have to walk in the shame of our addictions, or of our past. Our shame has been taken to the cross. We are now able to walk in victory over our past and all addictions.

Where does the power to overcome your addictions come from? The power comes from knowing who God is and who you are in Christ.

What a powerful truth. When we know God, we have a strength we can never attain on our own. The Word of God says, we, who know our God, will be made strong and be able to do exploits. Look at Daniel (11:32), "And such as do wickedly against the covenant shall he corrupt by flatteries: but the people that do know their God shall be strong, and do *exploits*."

Now listen to it (Daniel 11: 32) from other versions;

> With flattery he will corrupt those who have violated the covenant, but the people who know their God will firmly resist him. *(NIV)*

> He will flatter those who hate the things of God and win them over to his side. But the people who know their God shall be strong and do great things. *(TLB)*

> The king of the North will tell lies to God's people. Those who have not obeyed God will be ruined. But there will be some who know God and obey him. They will be strong and fight back. *(International Children's Bible)*

This will help you grasp the power in the Word of God! Allow it to energize you, to think that, "if I truly know God and trust Him, I will be strong and do great things." Speak it out, "I can do great things."

We can be successful. We can resist the enemy. We can be prosperous. We can be healed of sickness. We can overcome the bondage of our addictions. We can be more than a conqueror through Christ Jesus. We can walk in victory. Alleluia! Amen! All we need to do is get to know the One from whom our strength comes from. Amen!

We need to know Him and He will make us strong. And we will do what? We SHALL DO EXPLOITS. That means we will do remarkable, daring, and bold deeds. It means power over our addictions.

Come to believe one thing for sure now. If you are to be strong, successful, victorious, live a more abundant life, live the good Life, and be free your addictions, you must get to know God and trust in Him. Amen!

When we feel weak and feel like it's too much, (Proverbs 18:10):

_____

_____

_____

_____

He is our source of strength when the world seems to come down around us; when all seems to be lost; when you feel that there is no hope. When you feel that you have no strength left to fight, He is there as a strong tower to provide a safe refuge. Glory to God! Amen!

The Hebrew word for *safe* (in Proverbs 18:10) is *saw-gab*, which means to be inaccessible or safe. In everyday language it says, "you can't get at me." What God is saying is that when we trust in Him and walk in His Name, which is in His authority, we are literally made "too strong" to be overcome by the things of this world, the attacks of the enemy, or our addictions.

The truth of that Scripture re-enforces what Daniel (11:32) says, when we understand that trusting in the *name of the Lord* is trusting in the Lord Himself. When we know God we are strengthened and are safe in Him to do what He has called us to do. The word translated "strong" in Daniel means "to make stronger" or "to withstand."

We need to get this deep in our heart. God is the protector of the righteous. He takes His children and makes them safe in Himself and lifts you above the danger. He makes you capable of great exploits. You shall do great things. You can accomplish great things. You do not have to live a life of mediocrity. You can live God's kind of life. Alleluia!

You can stand safe, as a child of God who walks in the Name of the Lord having put your trust in Him as your strong tower. Then, you are, "too strong to be brought down." Amen!

As a child of God, when you know who you are in Christ and trust in Him, you are stronger than any problem that comes your way.

When we believe and act on the Word of God, when we get it in our hearts that our strength comes when we know God, then, no longer does it have to be; "maybe," "if only," "I'm not sure about," " I can't," "I just don't know about that," or any other statement of doubt or confession of unbelief. God's Word tells me that if I know Him, I will do great things.

I encourage you to take the word "can't" out of your vocabulary. Get to know God and you will then understand that, "If you can'?" said Jesus. "Everything is possible for him who believes." (Mark 9:23)

Because, "With man this is impossible, but not with God; all things are possible with God." (Mark 10:27).

We get to know God by turning our hearts away from our own ways, our own thinking, and by turning our lives over to God. Amen! If you haven't come to know Jesus as your Savior and Lord, then you truly cannot know God. Jesus said, *Then they asked him, "Where is your father?" "You do not know me or my Father," Jesus replied. "If you knew me, you would know my Father also."* (John 8:19)

If you want to know God, you must know Jesus, for He said, "I am the good shepherd; I know my sheep and my sheep know me— 15 just as the Father knows me and I know the Father—and I lay down my life for the sheep." (John 10:14-15)

Jesus laid down His life so that we may know the great I AM, God the Father. Are you willing to lay down your life to know Jesus and thus come to know the one true God? The One who makes you more than a conquerer, meets all your needs, heals all your diseases, and makes you the head and not the tail.

Once you turn your life over to God, it is then that you do as God instructs through Peter (2 Peter 3:18):

_____

_____

_____

This is accomplished when we begin to renew our minds as God also instructs us,

> Do not conform any longer to the pattern of this world, but be transformed by the renewing of your mind. Then you will be able to test and approve what God's will is—his good, pleasing and perfect will. (Romans 12:2)

It begins with getting to know God just the same way we get to know another person we want to know. We talk to the person, we listen to what they say, and we spend time with them.

It's the same with knowing God. We know Him by reading and studying His Word, spending time in prayer, listening to what He has to say, and fellowshipping with other brothers and sisters in the Lord. We know Him through His faithfulness and His mighty wonders of creation. We know Him when we call on Him and He is there to answer our every call. What an awesome God we serve. Because of His great love for His children, He made Himself known and continues to make Himself known to those who call on Him.

That's what this step is about, adding the knowledge of who God is and knowing who you are in Christ. This step is about building your, "Christ-esteem," not your self-esteem. I guarantee, if you know who you are in Christ, your self-esteem will be in proper perspective; *"For in him you have been enriched in every way—in all your speaking and in all your knowledge."* (1 Corinthians 1:5)

So, you might ask, "who is this God to whom I have given my life to do with what He so desires? What do I do now? Who am I Christ?" These questions will be answered in the following Bible study exercises.

Exercises for Step Three

Part One of Three—Relationship to God

Read the following Scriptures and *write down what you learn* about God and your relationship to Him.

(Romans 3:21-22): _____

_____

_____

_____

(Luke 15:1-32): _____

_____

_____

_____

(Psalm 32:1-2 and 2 Corinthians 5:19-20): _____

_____

_____

_____

_____

_____

(2 Corinthians 3:18): _____

_____

_____

(Romans 4:25 and 5:1): _____

_____

_____

_____

(Romans 9:30-33): _____

_____

_____

_____

_____

Part Two—God

Read the following Scriptures and *write down* the truth about God.

(Psalm 139:1-18): _____

_____

_____

_____

_____

_____

_____

_____

(Psalm 140:1-8): _____

_____

_____

_____

_____

_____

(Romans 15:7): _____

_____

_____

(Isaiah 40:11): _____

_____

_____

(Hebrews 13:6): _____
_____
_____

(Exodus 34:6; 2 Peter 3:9): _____
_____
_____
_____

(Jeremiah 31:3): _____
_____
_____

(John 10:7-18): _____
_____
_____
_____
_____

(Hebrews 4:15-16): _____
_____
_____
_____
_____

(Psalm 130:4): _____
_____
_____

(Luke 15:1-7): _____
_____
_____
_____
_____
_____
_____

(Romans 8:28-30): _____
_____
_____
_____
_____
_____
_____

God's Promise Fulfilled

Part Three—You

Who are you? Look up the following Scriptures and *write out* what the Word of God says about you.

(1 Corinthians 6:19-20): _____

_____

_____

(John 15:15): _____

_____

_____

(Romans 5:1): _____

_____

_____

(1 Corinthians 6:17): _____

_____

_____

_____

_____

(Ephesians 1:3-8): _____

_____

_____

_____

_____

(John 1:12): _____

_____

_____

(Romans 8:28): _____

_____

_____

(Colossians 1:13-14): _____

_____

_____

_____

_____

(Colossians 2:9-10): _____

_____

_____

_____

(Hebrews 4:14-16): _____

_____

_____

(Romans 8:1-2): _____

_____

_____

_____

(Romans 8:31-39): _____

_____

_____

_____

_____

_____

(2 Corinthians 1:21-22): _____

_____

(Colossians 3:1-4): _____

_____

_____

(Philippians 1:6): _____

_____

_____

(Philippians 3:20): _____

_____

(2 Timothy 1:7): _____

_____

_____

(1 John 5:18): _____

_____

_____

(John 15:5): _____

_____

_____

(John 15:16): _____

_____

_____

(1 Corinthians 3:16): _____

_____

_____

(Ephesians 2:6): _____

_____

_____

(Ephesians 2:10): _____

_____

_____

(Ephesians 3:12): _____

_____

_____

(2 Corinthians 5:17-21): _____
_____
_____
_____
_____
_____
_____

(Philippians 4:13): _____
_____
_____
_____

Chapter 7
Self-Control—Step 4

Now that you have a better awareness of Who God is and who you are in Christ, it is time to focus on a change of direction related to everyday life decisions. You have been the problem all along, and now it is time to make different choices; to repair broken relationships; to choose to be obedient to the Word of God.

This step is about reaching out and sharing the love of Christ through your own life. Instead of being controlled by your old nature and enslaved by the addictions that have controlled you for so many years, you now make a choice to walk in the power of the Holy Spirit, who gives you the ability and power to be self-controlled. No longer do you have to be in bondage to the compulsive behaviors of addiction, tormented by the guilt and shame of a destructive past.

The power of the Holy Spirit and Word of God give you the ability to walk in victory over your addictions. God has provided the power to walk in freedom. You remember the abuse of substances or other addictions are an act of your sinful nature listed in Galatians (5:21). These sinful behaviors are what so often lead to addiction and its bondage. However, Galatians (5:22-26) gives you the solution:

> But the fruit of the Spirit is love, joy, peace, patience, kindness, goodness, faithfulness, [23] gentleness and self-control. Against such things there is no law. [24] Those who belong to Christ Jesus have crucified the sinful nature with its passions and desires. [25] Since we live by the Spirit, let us keep in step with the Spirit. [26] Let us not become conceited, provoking and envying each other.

Your sinful nature has been crucified. As a child of God you are no longer a slave to your sinful nature, having to obey the compulsion to drink or use drugs. You can decide not to fulfill the desires of your old nature. You can choose to walk in the Spirit and not fulfill the desires of the sinful flesh.

What Do You Choose?

This may seem like an easy question. Then again, maybe it isn't so easy to answer. Maybe you're thinking, "what are my choices?" Perhaps you figure you have already made your choice. Or you may think, "I don't want to have to make choices about anything." Remember, not making a choice is still a choice.

At times, it seems like there are just too many things to choose from, or too many decisions to be made. But you know, that's how life is. There are choices and decisions for us to make. There really is no way around it. Amen!

God has given us the responsibility to make choices. He gives us choices to make. He has given us the freedom to choose. It is one of the greatest gifts we have been given. In fact, it may be the greatest gift. What does the Word of God have to say about choice?

In Deuteronomy we find that God is preparing His people to receive the gift of the Promised Land—the land flowing with milk and honey; the land where the promises of God will be realized, the land where God's people must make the choice to live in obedience to God's Word. Moses is preaching to a new generation in Israel. He is reminding them that the land they are about to enter is the gift God had promised. Look at Deuteronomy (30:15); *"See, I set before you today life and prosperity, death and destruction."*

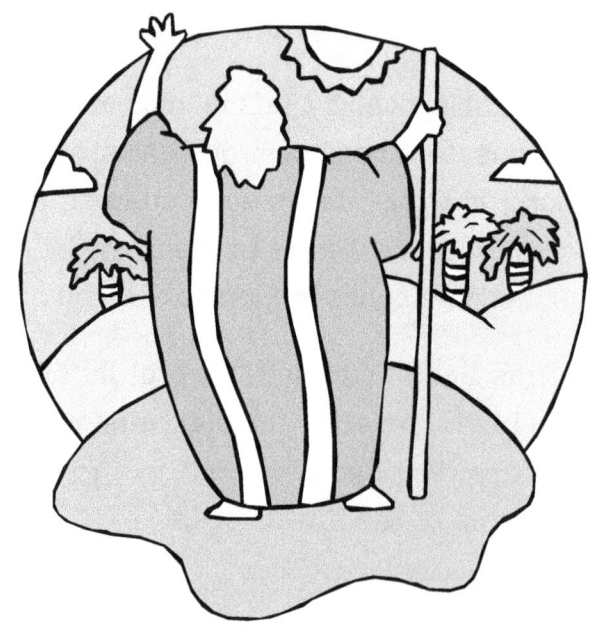

Moses is telling the children of God, as you enter the Promised Land, if you are going to experience God's gift to the fullest you must make choices. The gift the Israelites are about to take hold of requires it. And if Israel loves the Lord, is obedient to Him, and walks in His ways, they will be blessed.

God's gift included freedom from wandering—freedom from fear, hurt and need. It included a place where God promised He would provide for His children's every need—He promised His protection and His presence. However, as God's children we must understand something very important; the basis for the gift is not how good or great we were or we are, but an undeserved gift from a loving, faithful, awesome God. Our response is to live a life that honors God through gratitude, obedience to, and the fear (awe) of the Lord.

The words of Moses apply to us today. We are to make the choice. We are to make choices throughout our walk with the Lord, if we are to walk in the blessings of God. God has given the believer many gifts:

Healing

Later Jesus found him at the temple and said to him, "See, you are well again. Stop sinning or something worse may happen to you." [15] The man went away and told the Jews that it was Jesus who had made him well. (James 5:14-16)

Provision

And my God will meet all your needs according to his glorious riches in Christ Jesus. (Philippians 4:19)

Everlasting Life

For God so loved the world that he gave his one and only Son, that whoever believes in him shall not perish but have eternal life. (John 3:16)

There are many other Scriptures that speak of the promises of God. Paul was very aware of this when said to the Corinthian Church, (2 Corinthians 1:20):

_____

_____

_____

We also have a gift of which was previously mentioned. As I stated before, perhaps it is the greatest gift we have, and I suggest to you, it may be the one gift we should be the most careful to use.

The gift I am referring to is the freedom of choice—to be able to make decisions, to have free will. We as God's creation, can think, make decisions, and choose from right and wrong. We must choose between blessing and curse, between life and death. This gift is returned to us when we are in recovery. In fact, true freedom is being able to say NO. Amen!

In Step Three, it was that gift that was in operation when you made a decision to ask Jesus into your life, to be Lord and Savior of your life, to come into your heart. At that time you made a life-changing decision, a choice to live for Jesus, to stop being disobedient to God. You chose to live for Jesus and no longer the world or self

This freedom was given to us from the beginning, at God's creation of mankind. Man was given the ability to choose; to follow his own way and/or listen to the enemy, or man could listen to God and follow Him.

In chapter two of Genesis, we saw that after God created Adam and Eve, He placed them in the Garden; a place where they would fellowship with God. They were given everything they would need to live and be prosperous. Nothing was lacking. Then, God gave them a choice. They would be free to choose. They would now have to make a decision for the first time.

> The LORD God took the man and put him in the Garden of Eden to work it and take care of it. 16 And the LORD God commanded the man, "You are free to eat from any tree in the garden; 17 but you must not eat from the tree of the knowledge of good and evil, for when you eat of it you will surely die."
> (Genesis 2:15)

Until this time, man did not have to choose to follow God or to obey Him. Now man had to make a choice. He had something from which to choose. He could obey God and not eat of the tree of knowledge of good and evil, or disobey God and eat of the tree of knowledge of good and evil and die. To show you that this was truly a matter of freedom of choice, let's take a close look at what happened.

The problem man had was not that he did not know what he was to do or not to do, it was that he did not obey God. Through this one act of disobedience, death, both spiritual and physical, was brought into the world. Ever since the fall, man's problem has not been not knowing what he should do—he has God's Word to know what to do—but the problem is his not being obedient to that Word. Amen!

We see from this one act of disobedience that sin entered the world and we are all were affected by this one event. This is explained in Romans (5:19):

_____

_____

_____

_____

Just as all are affected by one sin, all sin is affected by one. God, because of His great love for us, provided a way for us to be restored to right fellowship with Him. In the fullness of time, at the right moment, He sent His son, Jesus. One who would restore fellowship, bring forgiveness, supply power to live an over coming life, and reconcile us to the Father—something we could not do ourselves. This is what Christianity is about. The Father's gift of Jesus is the substance of the Christian Life.

The Father's sending of Jesus makes Christianity different from other religions of the world. Other religions offer a different system. They offer a do-it-yourself system. They tell you, if you just be a good person, follow a good lifestyle, or seek a higher plain you will find favor with god, and may eventually achieve salvation or relocate to Paradise. In other religions, good works are performed in order to receive a reward (e.g. in order to get to heaven one must do this or that). In Christianity good works are "a therefore." (See: Colossians 3:12 and Romans 12:1.)

In other religions, good works are seen as a means to salvation. Christianity is the only religion that offers assurance of salvation. In Christianity, salvation is received as a free gift. *"For it is by grace you have been saved, through faith—and this not from yourselves, it is the gift of God—⁹ not by works, so that no one can boast."* (Ephesians 2:8-9) Christ also gives us forgiveness, cleanses us of sin, and makes us the righteousness of God through Him.

Other religions say, "what must I do?" And Christianity is; "it is finished." It depends on what God has done for us and given to us, not on what we do or how many good works we can do. If it were based on works, how would anyone know when he or she had done enough? We would never know.

God has provided a way, the only way, his Son Jesus Christ. He is the Way, the Truth, and the Life. In this, we have an assurance of our salvation through faith in Him. It is through Christ that we have the ability to refuse to eat from the tree of The Knowledge of Good and Evil, and choose to eat of the Tree of Life. Amen!

We have the ability to choose blessing or curse, life or death. We have the freedom to choose to be obedient or disobedient. In Christ, we have been given the mind of Christ. With the mind of Christ, we make decisions about life. Every day we are faced with any number of situations with circumstances that require us to make a choice. Some circumstances require easy decisions, others may present much more difficult choices. The decisions often become harder, but we can always make the best choice possible with the help of the Holy Spirit. If we are not sure, we ask for wisdom to make the right decision. James tell us what to do when we lack wisdom. He tells us (James 1:5-8):

> ⁵ If any of you lacks wisdom, he should ask God, who gives generously to all without finding fault, and it will be given to him. ⁶ But when he asks, he must believe and not doubt, because he who doubts is like a wave of the sea, blown and tossed by the wind. ⁷ That man should not think he will receive anything from the Lord; ⁸ he is a double-minded man, unstable in all he does.

We don't have to be afraid in making decisions. It is what God wants us to do. God has given us the ability to do it. Why do we have freedom of choice? So we can make the choice to be obedient and walk in the Spirit, to again walk in the cool of the day with God. Amen!

How do we continue to improve on making right choices, to walk in obedience to God's Word? It is through the renewing of our minds. (Romans 12:1-2)

As we renew our minds to the Word of God, we will be able to discern the will of God for our lives. Do you remember how Paul struggled with this? He tells us in Romans (7:15-24) of his trying to do what God wants him to do:

> I do not understand what I do. For what I want to do I do not do, but what I hate I do. ¹⁶ And if I do what I do not want to do, I agree that the law is good. ¹⁷ As it is, it is no longer I myself who do it, but it is sin living in me. ¹⁸ I know that nothing good lives in me, that is, in my sinful nature. For I have the desire to do what is good, but I cannot carry it out. ¹⁹ For what I do is not the good I want to do; no, the evil I do not want to do—this I keep on doing.
>
> ²⁰ Now if I do what I do not want to do, it is no longer I who do it, but it is sin living in me that does it. ²¹ So I find this law at work: When I want to do good, evil is right there with me. ²² For in my inner being I delight in God's law; ²³ but I see another law at work in the members of my body, waging war against the law of my mind and making me a prisoner of the law of sin at work within my members. ²⁴ What a wretched man I am! Who will rescue me from this body of death? ²⁵ Thanks be to God—through Jesus Christ our Lord! So then, I myself in my mind am a slave to God's law, but in the sinful nature a slave to the law of sin.

And then in Romans 7 verse 25 Paul declares:

_____

_____

_____

_____

_____

It is with his mind that he is able to choose to be obedient to God.

This is how we will be able to walk in obedience to the Word of God. With the mind of Christ we will be able to choose that which brings glory to God. Our life will reflect the awesome love of God for his children. It is with the mind of Christ and the Power of the Holy Spirit that we will walk by faith and not by sight, and therefore be pleasing to God. *"And without faith it is impossible to please God, because anyone who comes to him must believe that he exists and that he rewards those who earnestly seek him."* (Hebrews 11:6)

It is at this step that your history as an alcoholic or drug addict is left behind. You now develop a new history, a history that includes recovery. In recovery, your past is just that, the past. Who you were is just that, who you were. Who you are in Christ is who you are now. Thus, you can make people aware of who you were, but they can *know* who you are now. They will know you by your fruit.

You are set free to repair damaged relationships, your own reputation, the way people see you. It is now that you can choose to break down the strongholds in your life and put away resentments you have held onto for so long. You can now begin to reach out to others, and give of yourself instead of taking from everyone else. It is a choice to make that will make all the difference in the world.

I want to tell you about a time I was at a church service. I was in the prayer line, behind another person. When asked by the preacher what she wanted prayer for, she said to him, "I want you to pray that God make all my decisions for me so I would do what God wants me to do." I said to myself, please don't pray that prayer. In the end, the preacher did not pray as she had asked him.

That is not what God has asked of you. It is not found anywhere in the Word of God that He is going to make all your decisions for you. No, wisdom has been given to us so that we are to choose to be obedient. We are to exercise our freedom of choice. Remember what Moses said to the people of God as they were about to enter the promise of God. Those words are echoed today.

> [15] See, I set before you today life and prosperity, death and destruction. [16] For I command you today to love the LORD your God, to walk in his ways, and to keep his commands, decrees and laws; then you will live and increase, and the LORD your God will bless you in the land you are entering to possess.
>
> [17] But if your heart turns away and you are not obedient, and if you are drawn away to bow down to other gods and worship them, [18] I declare to you this day that you will certainly be destroyed. You will not live long in the land you are crossing the Jordan to enter and possess.

[19] This day I call heaven and earth as witnesses against you that I have set before you life and death, blessings and curses. Now choose life, so that you and your children may live [20] and that you may love the LORD your God, listen to his voice, and hold fast to him. For the LORD is your life, and he will give you many years in the land he swore to give to your fathers, Abraham, Isaac and Jacob. (Deuteronomy 30:15-20)

Step 4 Exercises

The tasks and exercises for Step 4 are extensive. There are six different requirements and they will take some time and effort.

Step 4—Task 1: One-On-One Discussions

The first exercise for Step 4 is to conduct a one-on-one discussion with every member of your group. The questions below will be asked of each member and discussed. You will then write a brief paragraph about what you learned and turn it in to your facilitator. Use separate sheets of paper for each paragraph. The questions you should ask each group member are:

1. How did you come to be in this group?

2. What are your goals in life?

3. How do you see God working in your life now?

4. How has your life changed since entering Program?

5. How has your relationship with God changed since entering the Program?

Step 4—Task 2: Helping Others

The second thing you must do is document (in writing) a minimum of 10 hours of where you helped someone and received nothing in return. This cannot be for a relative. I suggest this be at a mission, church, or a community agency that reaches out to the poor, disabled, or elderly. Use the space below to list what you did for the 10 hours, noting the date and times.

My 10 Hours Helping Others
Activity/Date/Hours

Step 4—Task 3: Important Relationships in My Life

In this exercise you will look at the important relationships in your life. Think about the nature of the relationship, any damage that might have occurred in it, how damage can be repaired, and the goals you have in each relationship. We begin with the most important relationship we have: Our relationship with God.

1. God:

My relationship with God in the present: _____

What did I do to damage that relationship? _____

_____

How can I repair my relationship with God? _____

_____

What is my goal in this relationship? _____

_____

When will I do this? _____

2. Other person: _____

My relationship to them: _____

_____

How have I damaged this relationship? _____

_____

How can I repair the damage and improve this relationship? _____

_____

What is my goal in this relationship? _____

_____

When will I do this? _____

3. Other person: _____

My relationship to them: _____

_____

How have I damaged this relationship? _____

_____

How can I repair the damage and improve this relationship? _____

_____

What is my goal in this relationship? _____

_____

When will I do this? _____

4. Other person: _____

My relationship to them: _____

_____

How have I damaged this relationship? _____

_____

How can I repair the damage and improve this relationship? _____

_____

What is my goal in this relationship? _____

_____

When will I do this? _____

5. Other person: _____

My relationship to them: _____

_____

How have I damaged this relationship? _____

_____

How can I repair the damage and improve this relationship? _____

_____

What is my goal in this relationship? _____

_____

When will I do this? _____

6. Other person: _____

My relationship to them: _____
_____

How have I damaged this relationship? _____
_____

How can I repair the damage and improve this relationship? _____
_____

What is my goal in this relationship? _____
_____

When will I do this? _____

Step 4—Task 4: **With God/Without God**

In this exercise, you are to first identify five times in your life where you can see that God was working in your life. Take your time doing this. Try to look over your life and find the most significant times where you are able to see you and God working together (from as early in your life as you can remember to the present), and decide on the top five. Describe them below.

1. _____

2. _____

3. _____

4. _____

5. _____

Next, you are to identify the five times in your life that you were doing things without God (i.e. on your own). Take your time with this. Describe them below.

1. _____

2. _____

3. _____

4. _____

5. _____

Now, consider the times in your life with God. What was the outcome of these situations? Who else was involved? How did you feel toward others and God? What feelings did you experience? How were you co-operating with God?

Now, consider the times in your life where you were not working with God. What was it like not working with God? Who else was involved? How did you feel toward others and God? What feelings did you experience?

Step 4—Task 5: **Circle of Relationships**

1. Draw a picture that represents the biggest relationship problem in your life now.
2. Draw a picture of the biggest problem, or difficulty in that relationship.
3. Draw a picture of the biggest problem in your relationship with God now.
4. Draw a picture of something you dislike doing with other people, but must do anyway.
5. Draw a picture of something you like to do with another person.
6. Draw a picture of something you believe God is directing you to do now.
7. Draw a picture of the most important person in your life, other than yourself.
8. Draw a picture of the special relationship in life that you believe will lead you to happiness.

In the center, draw a picture that represents your relationship with God. That is, draw something that shows how you feel towards God now.

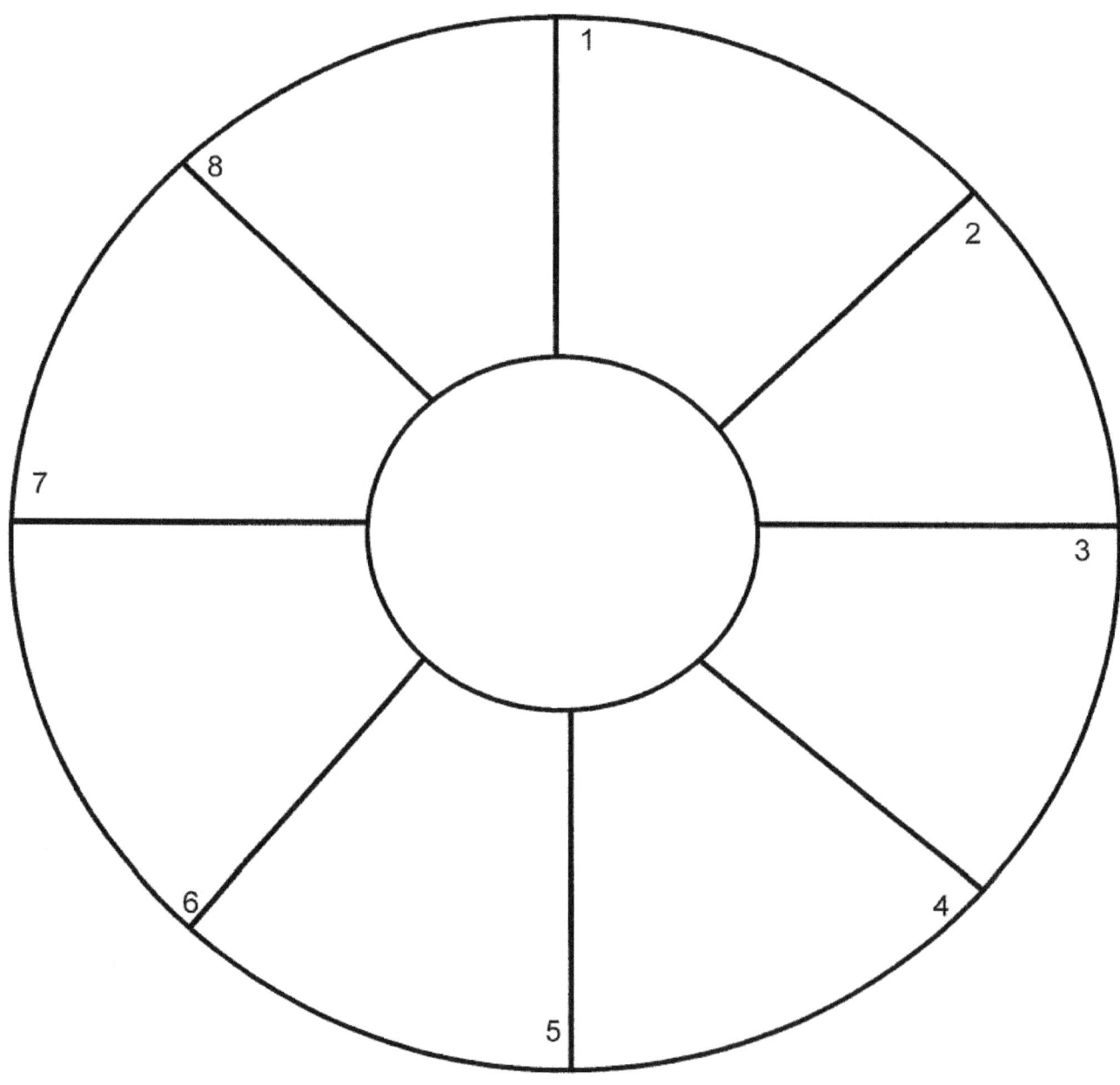

Step 4—Task 6: Trading Places

In this exercise, you are to identify someone you would like to trade places with. Someone you would like to be (temporarily). You must identify someone. Carefully think about this. You will share this, and some of the other exercises in group.

Person I'd Trade Places With: _____

Next, you are to identify the four important things about that person that would make you want to be that person. List the four items in order of their importance, number one being the most important item, and so on.

1. _____

2. _____

3. _____

4. _____

Chapter 8
Perseverance—Step 5

Our source of authority is the Word of God. It is our final authority. Or, may I say, it is my "Final Answer." If you are a believer, then, the Word tells us we are to walk by faith and not by sight. Amen!

(2 Corinthians 5:7): _____

_____

_____

We exercise faith in our lives quite often. Have you ever thought about how big a part faith plays in our everyday affairs? It takes faith to get married because marriage vows are promises. It takes faith to send children off to school. It takes faith to get a prescription filled. It takes faith to eat in a restaurant, deposit money in a bank, sign a contract, drive on the highway, get on an airplane or an elevator, or sit in a chair. Do you see? Faith isn't some kind of religious experience for the super spiritual; it's the glue that holds people's lives together.

Step Five is about persevering. Our faith in Christ and knowing who you are in Him is the means by which we are able to endure, to overcome the struggles of addiction, and to persevere in life. It is when we meditate on God's Word, both day

and night, and fellowship with people who believe the Word of God and encourage us, that we are made strong. Our faith is increased to face the trials of life, or speak to our mountain—and command it to move. We are able to move that mountain or perhaps, if need be, climb it. Whether I need to move a mountain or climb it, as a believer, when I persevere; "I am more than a conqueror." Amen!

We must remember faith is only as good as its object. If we trust people, we get what people can do. If we trust money, we get what money can do. If we trust ourselves, we get what we can do. If we trust God, we get what God can do. Glory to God! As a believer and not a doubter, I choose to put my faith in God and His Word and walk in His promises.

The truth is that, without God and His promises revealed in His Word, there is no hope. And without hope there is nothing for which to persevere for. Ephesians (2:10-12) tells us:

> Therefore, remember that formerly you who are Gentiles by birth and called "uncircumcised" by those who call themselves "the circumcision" (that done in the body by the hands of men)—¹² remember that at that time you were separate from Christ, excluded from citizenship in Israel and foreigners to the covenants of the promise, without hope and without God in the world.
>
> ¹³ But now in Christ Jesus you who once were far away have been brought near through the blood of Christ. ¹⁴ For he himself is our peace, who has made the two one and has destroyed the barrier, the dividing wall of hostility, ¹⁵ by abolishing in his flesh the law with its commandments and regulations. His purpose was to create in himself one new man out of the two, thus making peace, ¹⁶ and in this one body to reconcile both of them to God through the cross, by which he put to death their hostility.
>
> ¹⁷ He came and preached peace to you who were far away and peace to those who were near. ¹⁸ For through him we both have access to the Father by one Spirit. ¹⁹ Consequently, you are no longer foreigners and aliens, but fellow citizens with God's people and members of God's household, ²⁰ built on the foundation of the apostles and prophets, with Christ Jesus himself as the chief cornerstone. ²¹ In him the whole building is joined together and rises to become a holy temple in the Lord. ²² And in him you too are being built together to become a dwelling in which God lives by his Spirit.

Alleluia! The Word became flesh. Jesus now lives in the heart of the believer and through His shed blood, we have been given hope and are brought back into a right relationship with God the Father. We are no longer separated from God. No, in Christ we have the Hope of Glory (Colossians 1:27). Amen!

So, where do we turn? Where does the believer go? We always go directly to the Word of God. No other source is as sure and true, or has the authority for the believer to stand on. We know this because God tells us (Romans 10:17) that:

___

___

___

Our faith is built-up when we spend time in the Word.

Have you come to a place in your life where you are ready to step out as a believer, and not doubt the Words of your one true friend—Jesus? He's the best friend you have, and He is always there reaching out His hand and lifting you to safety. Or, as His Word says, "he restores my soul. He guides me in paths of righteousness for his name's sake." (Psalm 23:3).

You just have to believe, and not doubt that you can reach the safe place where He is standing. You have to believe that He is able to keep you free from the addiction— to strengthen you so you are able to refuse to give in to the temptations of Satan and the negative thoughts that come to your mind.

We come to that faith level when we take God's Word for what He says it is. We must understand that God says what He means and means what He says—Amen! His Word is true, pure, and never fails. We must believe that God's Word is His will. Because it is His will, we can be confident that He is there each step of the way. We have His Word on it.

> This is the confidence we have in approaching God: that if we ask anything according to his will, he hears us. [15] And if we know that he hears us—whatever we ask—we know that we have what we asked of him. (1 John 5:14-15)

Are you ready to step to the level God is calling you to? To rise up to the higher ground where a friend who has given you all you need for life, is waiting for you to decide to live like a believer and not a doubter? Are you ready to live the life of a believer? To live in the reality of God's Word and live in knowing who you are as a child of God?

The Word of God says who you are: Look up the Scriptures below and only write what or who it states you are according to God.

(I Peter 1:23):

(John 17:21-23):

(I John 5:4):

(Ephesians 6:10):

(I Corinthians 2:16):

(Ephesians 2:6):

(I Peter 2:24):

(Revelation 21:7):

(Colossians 2:7):

(2 Corinthians 2:14):

(Ephesians 5:1):

This is what we are and who we are in Christ. Amen! As believers, we stand on the authority of God's Word. We stand on the authority of the Name of Jesus. We are to stand in that authority and use the Name of Jesus, and expect what God has said will be. Listen to what Jesus says to us, "And I will do whatever you ask in my name, so that the Son may bring glory to the Father." (John 14:13)

I encourage you today to begin to confess the Word with your mouth and believe His words to you. Remember what Mark (11:23-25) tells us: if we don't doubt, believe in our hearts, ask, pray, and speak the truth, we will be able to move mountains.

In all of this, and throughout the day, praise God continually. Offer the sacrifice of praise, and walk in love. Through Jesus, therefore, let us continually offer to God a sacrifice of praise—the fruit of lips that confess his name. "And do not forget to do good and to share with others, for with such sacrifices God is pleased." (Hebrews 13:15-16)

Are you ready to reach up for the hand of God and live as a believer? Are you ready to trust Him who is able to do more than we can imagine? (Ephesians 3:20)

Are you ready to look beyond the moment and dare to desire all that God has for you in recovery? His words of encouragement will strengthen you.

(1 Timothy 4:16): _____

_____

_____

Are you ready to let go of the past, to die to self and stand on the promises of God? Then take your stand and walk in the power of the Holy Spirit until the Lord's return. Read what Hebrews (10:35-38) says to us:

> So do not throw away your confidence; it will be richly rewarded. [36] You need to persevere so that when you have done the will of God, you will receive what he has promised. [37] For in just a very little while, "He who is coming will come and will not delay. [38] But my righteous one will live by faith. And if he shrinks back, I will not be pleased with him."

What a tremendous promise. When we cooperate with God—walk in the Spirit—we can persevere and *walk in victory* over the darkness of addiction and all the pain and suffering related to a life of bondage to sin.

This step is about letting go of what you want and giving up the way you think the world is or should be. In the beginning of this workbook we talked about reality. You learned that what the world says is reality, and what God says is real, are usually in direct opposition to each other. Remember, Jesus is the Truth. When Jesus said in John (14:6) "He was the Truth," He was telling us He is REALITY. If we want to live in reality—NOT in Virtual Reality, as the world lives—we will walk with Jesus, and not with the world.

If you are ready, go with this word of encouragement: *"Humble yourselves, therefore, under God's mighty hand, that he may lift you up in due time. ⁷ Cast all your anxiety on him because he cares for you."* (1 Peter 5:6-7)

Step 5 Exercises

There are 5 written exercises for Step 5. Take your time when completing them. When you are finished, meet with your counselor and go over your responses. None of the exercises for this step are shared in group.

Step 5—Task 1: One Year to Live

In this series of exercises you will begin envisioning your life in recovery. To identify your goals, both short-term and long-term, think about your gifts and how you will live a godly life. You will set your "real" goals shortly, but in these first three exercises, you have been given background information that might change things.

One Year to Live

You have found out you have only one year to live. You will not experience any pain. There is no cure. No miracle can save you. You are going to die. Your task is to identify the things that you want to accomplish in the next year. Think about it and write them below.

1. _____
2. _____
3. _____
4. _____
5. _____
6. _____
7. _____
8. _____
9. _____
10. _____

93

Step 5—Task 2: Five Years to Live

You have found out you have only five years to live. You will not experience any pain. There is no cure. No miracle can save you. You are going to die. Your task is to identify the things that you want to accomplish in the next 5 years. Think about it and write them below.

1. _____
2. _____
3. _____
4. _____
5. _____
6. _____
7. _____
8. _____
9. _____
10. _____

Step 5—Task 3: Ten Years to Live

You have found out you have only ten years to live. You will not experience any pain. There is no cure. No miracle can save you. You are going to die. Your task is to identify the things that you want to accomplish in the next 10 years. Think about it and write them below.

1. _____
2. _____
3. _____
4. _____
5. _____
6. _____
7. _____
8. _____
9. _____
10. _____

Step 5—Task 4: Master Vision Plan

After you have completed the one-year, five-year, and ten-year to live exercises, you should be ready to form some "real" goals that reflect a decision to live in sobriety and maintain a "godly" life. This is called your Master Vision Plan. It consists of one, five, and ten-year goals.

One Year Master Vision Plan

Date Today:_____

One Year Completion Date:_____

1. I will: _____

2. I will: _____

3. I will: _____

4. I will: _____

5. I will: _____

6. I will: _____

7. I will: _____

8. I will: _____

9. I will: _____

10. I will: _____

Five Year Master Vision Plan

Date Today:_____

Five Year Completion Date:_____

1. I will: _____

2. I will: _____

3. I will: _____

4. I will: _____

5. I will: _____

6. I will: _____

7. I will: _____

8. I will: _____

9. I will: _____

10. I will: _____

Ten Year Master Vision Plan

Date Today:_____

Ten Year Completion Date:_____

1. I will: _____

2. I will: _____

3. I will: _____

4. I will: _____

5. I will: _____

6. I will: _____

7. I will: _____

8. I will: _____

9. I will: _____

10. I will: _____

Step 5—Task 5: Action Plan

The final Exercise for Step 5 is called an *Action Plan*. It is a list of details and behavioral actions that are necessary for you to complete the goals you outlined in your *One Year Vision Plan*. In essence, the Action Plan answers the question, "What are the specific things I need to do to complete my One Year Goals?" List these things using as much detail as you can and try to include a timetable where specific dates are mentioned. This exercise forms a commitment to your vision for yourself.

Chapter 9
Godliness—Step 6

Be imitators of God, therefore, as dearly loved children ²and live a life of love, just as Christ loved us and gave himself up for us as a fragrant offering and sacrifice to God. (Ephesians 5:1-2)

Thus far your journey has brought you to a new life, a new way of thinking, setting goals and committing to reach those goals. Now, you have come to the step that puts it all on the table. Here you are required to start the process of walking the walk, and living what you have committed to in the preceding steps.

This step is adding godliness to your walk. It is about living the way God wants you to live, and not your way anymore. This is where sobriety becomes a way of life. This is the step where others are included in your new walk, goals, and hopes and dreams for the future. This is where you take the risk of trusting God, yourself, and others. Here, you begin the adventure of a lifetime.

What am I talking about? It is here that we add Godliness to our walk up the Victory Ladder. You are called to be an imitator of God, or, as said above in verse two, we are to live, "just as." I understand that it specifically states in the passage above that we are to live a life of love. But I want to show you that the Word of God calls us to live, do, speak, love, receive, and be "just as" God.

Now let me make it perfectly clear. I am not saying we are to be God. What I'm saying is that we are called to be "just as" He is. Amen!

What we are going to look at are some of the ways God has called us to be "just as" He is, ways that reflect God rightly, rather than presenting a false image of our Heavenly Father. Now, we're only going to look at a few of the many scriptures that tell us how we can be "just as" God wants us to be, because there are far too many references for us to address all of them.

The term used in Ephesians (5:2) and translated as "just as," is also translated in various other versions as: "and," "also," "so," or "even as." Thus, if we were to look at every reference we would be here quite a long time. So, let's get back to our foundation Scripture for this step.

We are told in verse one to be "Imitators." And in verse two, this is reinforced by the words "just as." Before we look at the Word to see how we are to be "just as" God, I want to give you some definitions that will help you understand exactly what we are called to be.

The first definition is "imitator." To be an imitator is to "seek to follow the example of; take as one's model or pattern, to act the same as; impersonate; mimic, to reproduce in form, color, etc., make a duplicate or copy of, to be or become like in appearance; resemble."

The second definition is the word "as." When we put the word "as" after the word "just," it means to the same amount or degree; equally, as in, "I'm just *as* happy at home as I am at church." As it says in Ephesians (5:1-2), "be imitators, just as, impersonate, mimic, become a copy, resemble, or model God." Saints, it can't be any clearer, we are to be "just as" God—in everything we think, say, or do. Amen!

One more thing needs to be made clear before we look at some of the ways God calls us to be "just as" He is. When God gives us instruction (commands us to be, think, say or do anything), we must understand that we cannot do it without His help. We must understand that without Him nothing is possible. There is no way that we can be anything like Him on our own, or by our own efforts. Amen. But, with Him, everything is possible (Mark 9:23).

Jesus Himself said what we can't do, God can do (Luke 18:27). Glory to God and Amen! What an awesome God we serve, that He would call his children to be "just as" He is and then enable us to do so through the work of the Holy Spirit.

But you ask, is it true? Oh, how can I be sure? I urge you. No, I beg you, look to your Heavenly Father's love letter to you, His word of love to you, and believe as Paul so bluntly tells us:

> [18] And we, who with unveiled faces all reflect the Lord's glory, are being transformed into his likeness with ever-increasing glory, which comes from the Lord, who is the Spirit. (2 Corinthians 3:18)

We must grasp this truth that God still walks on this earth in the person of the believer. He has made his home in us. That is, if you are a believer in His Son. If not, I'm not referring to you. God has chosen to live in us and because of this He calls us to be "just as" He is. So what are some of the ways in which we are to be "just as" God.

First, we can look right at today's Scripture and see that we are to live a life of love, *just as* Christ loved us and gave Himself up for us. Our life, what others see in us, is the love of God reflected in all that we are. People should see God in us. Living a life motivated by love means helping others see God as a loving Father, sharing the Gospel of Jesus Christ. It means becoming someone's friend, not judging others before you know something about them. It's being merciful.

It's sharing a smile and greeting others when you pass them by, or when greeted by someone. It's visiting the neighbor who is unable to get out because of age or illness. It is reading the Bible to someone unable to read, or conducting a Bible study for a person or group unable to go to church.

It means, *"Therefore each of you must put off falsehood and speak truthfully to his neighbor, for we are all members of one body,"* (Ephesians 4:25), and not harboring anger (Ephesians. 4:26). It is not speaking down to others, but lifting them up with words of encouragement, words that help them. (Ephesians 4:29). It means to live a Christ-like life:

> Therefore, as God's chosen people, holy and dearly loved, clothe yourselves with compassion, kindness, humility, gentleness and patience. [13] Bear with each other and forgive whatever grievances you may have against one another. Forgive as the Lord forgave you. (Colossians 3:12-13)

To clothe ourselves, means literally to put on these attributes in the same way you would put on clothes before facing the world. As Paul puts it (Ephesians 4:32), "Be kind and compassionate to one another, forgiving each other, just as in Christ God forgave you." There you see another "just as."

This "just as" —at times—may be one of the hardest things we are called to do. For when we have been wronged, or believe that we have been wronged, forgiveness doesn't seem to come so easy. And for most of us that is extended to forgiving ourselves as well.

Remember, however, that we have the strength to forgive (Philippians 4:13). So, just as God forgives us of all our sin through Christ, we can forgive through the love of Christ that lives in us. Amen!

Even another biblical "Just as'" is, *"But just as he who called you is holy, so be holy in all you do;"* (1 Peter 1:15). Yes, we are called to be holy just as God is holy.

But you might reply, "How can I do this?" You say, "I can't be holy like God is holy, that's too much to ask of me." In and of yourself you cannot, but with Christ in you, you can. If we are to live a holy life, we must turn our lives over to Christ so He can turn our lives around. When we decide to turn our back on sin that destroys, He turns us back to the holiness of God. Amen!

Saints, when God chose to live in us He brought His holiness with Him, and He now calls on us to be holy. What He calls us to do is to chose a life of obedience, to follow Christ as our example, to be "just as" Christ is. Jesus lived a life without sin. And through His death and resurrection we are no longer slaves to the acts of our sinful nature. We have been made righteous through the blood of Christ. Amen!

With what, or to whom, can we compare God's holiness? The God of Abraham, Isaac and Jacob, and the Christian church is holy—He sets the standard. No other god worshiped or made with our own hands is like Him. Our God is merciful and just. He cares personally for each of His children.

He expects us to imitate Him through faith and obedience in all we do. For, it is through faith that we please Him and through obedience we are made holy.

(Hebrews 11:6): _____

_____

_____

_____

_____

_____

Our standard for holy living is God's holiness. Holiness means being set apart, totally devoted or dedicated to God. We're to be set apart and different, not conformed to the standards of the world.

What makes us different is having the attributes of God in our life. It's having the fruit of the Spirit evident in our everyday lives. Yes, it means having:

> But the fruit of the Spirit is love, joy, peace, patience, kindness, goodness, faithfulness, 23 gentleness and self-control. Against such things there is no law. 24 Those who belong to Christ Jesus have crucified the sinful nature with its passions and desires. (Galatians 5:22-24)

Walking in holiness means, as Christians, we have been called to walk in a love that is:

> If I speak in the tongues of men and of angels, but have not love, I am only a resounding gong or a clanging cymbal. 2 If I have the gift of prophecy and can fathom all mysteries and all knowledge, and if I have a faith that can move mountains, but have not love, I am nothing. 3 If I give all I possess to the poor and surrender my body to the flames, but have not love, I gain nothing.
>
> 4 Love is patient, love is kind. It does not envy, it does not boast, it is not proud. 5 It is not rude, it is not self-seeking, it is not easily angered, it keeps no record of wrongs. 6 Love does not delight in evil but rejoices with the truth. 7 It always protects, always trusts, always hopes, always perseveres. 8 Love never fails... (1 Corinthians 13:1-8)

Our highest priority and our single focus must be His. I know that sounds like a tall order, something impossible to achieve and such a contrast to our old nature and ways. Remember that God has given us His Holy Spirit, who has the power to enable us to overcome sin and walk in obedience. Thus, enabling us to be holy as He is holy! Amen!

Whatever you do, don't use the excuse that you can't help slipping into sin. I said it before, and I'll say it again. Take "can't" out of your vocabulary, because Jesus gives us the strength to stay clean and sober. Say this with me, "I can be free of sin, walk in righteousness, and remain clean and sober." Yes, you can, because you are set apart to live as a reflection of God and all He is. Amen!

Before we present the Step 6 exercises, on the next page, look up these additional Scripture references and write down the "just as" to help you be who or what God has called you to be.

(Hebrews 4:10): _____

(John 10:14-15): _____

(Ephesians 5:25): _____

(1 John 3:7): _____

(Hebrews 4:15): _____

(Colossians 2:6): _____

(Romans 6:4): _____

There are many more references. I encourage you to study the Word of God and see for yourself how God sees you, and what He has for you. Then, you will see yourself the way God sees you.

Let's look at one more verse (Revelation 3:21-22):

> *To him who overcomes, I will give the right to sit with me on my throne, just as I overcame and sat down with my Father on his throne. ²² He who has an ear, let him hear what the Spirit says to the churches."*

There is no literal portrait of Jesus that exists. But the likeness of the Son who sets us free will be seen in the lives of those who live out the life of His Son.

Step 6 Exercises

There are 5 written exercises for Step 6. Take your time when completing them. When you are finished, meet with your counselor and go over your responses. Only one of the exercises for this step is shared in group.

Step 6—Task 1: Update Action Plan

The first exercise for this step is to update your Action Plan. This will be review with your facilitator. Here is what you do for this. On pages 98-100 you wrote an Action Plan. It detailed the things you needed to do to fulfill your One-Year goals. Some time has passed since you wrote that Plan. Maybe it's just a week, or perhaps it's a month. At this moment in time, you are being asked to see if you are on track doing the things necessary to fulfill the goals and tasks you listed back on pages 98-100. You will meet with your facilitator and review what you wrote back then and what you have done—or not done. In the meeting you will bring the Plan up-to-date. It may sound complicated, but it isn't. It is simply a check-up to encourage you to keep on track.

Step 6—Task 2: Helping Others

The second exercise or task for this Step is to help others just as you did back in Step 4. You must document *an additional 10 hours* of doing something for someone,

receiving nothing in return. This cannot be for a relative. I suggest this be at a mission, church, or a community agency that reaches out to the poor, disabled, or elderly. Use the form on the next page to document the things you do.

Step 6—Task 3: Trading Places

This is a repeat of a Step 4 exercise, but you may choose to change the person you identify. In this exercise, you are to identify someone you would like to trade places with. Someone you would like to be (temporarily). You must identify someone. Carefully think about this. You will share this and some of the other exercises in group.

Person I'd Trade Places With: _____

Next, you are to identify the four important things about that person that would make you want to be that person. List the four items in order of their importance, number one being the most important item, and so on.

1. _____
2. _____
3. _____
4. _____

Step 6—Task 4: **Moral Assessment**

The final two exercises for this step begin with a moral assessment of what is in your life. This is based on what you learned in Step 3 concerning who God is and who you are in Christ. How has knowing the truth of who God is and who you are in Christ changed your thinking, feelings, and behavior?

You should start by briefly answering this question: *How have you implemented this knowledge into your everyday life?* Use the form below to write out a brief answer.

Next, to complete this Moral Assessmant task, you should briefly answer the following questions:

1. Do you find yourself lying to people? _____
_____

2. Do you find yourself cheating or stealing? _____
_____

3. Do you mislead people? _____
_____

4. Do you say things to people to hurt them or put them down? _____
_____

5. Do you treat people in ways you would not want to be treated? _____
_____

6. Do you betray confidences? _____
_____

7. Do you betray trust? _____
_____

8. Do you make excuses? _____
_____

9. Do you fail to help others? _____
_____

10. Are you using drugs or drinking? _____
_____

11. Are you overeating or starving yourself? _____
_____

12. Are you doing things that are physically or mentally unhealthy? _____
_____

13. Are the people in your life positive or negative? _____
_____

14. Are you taking control of all the things you need to? _____

15. Are you cutting corners at work or relationships? _____

16. Are you giving to others in your life? _____

17. Are you trying to control things that are not in your control? _____

18. Are you allowing others to influence you to do things you shouldn't do? _____

19. Are you treating other races or sexes with respect? _____

20. Do you make fun of others? _____

21. Do you manipulate others? _____

22. Do you turn your back on the needs of others? _____

23. Do you lead others astray? _____

24. Do you lose your temper? _____

25. Are you fair and honest in your dealings with others? _____

26. Do you show others respect? _____

27. Do you respect the rights of others? _____

28. Do you deny or admit your mistakes? _____
_____

29. Are you sharing your relationship with God with others? _____
_____

30. Are you attending a church, prayer meeting, or Bible study? _____
_____

31. Do you encourage others? _____
_____

32. Are you forgiving others? _____
_____

33. Are you forgiving yourself? _____
_____

This exercise will help you identify areas you need to correct and work on to improve. These are areas in your life that you have not committed to God so you can change and be more like He is. In general, by looking over the answers you gave to the 33 questions above, you will find core problem areas. In the last task of this Step, you are to decide on five areas where you need to focus and make improvements. After you have identified these five areas of concern, make a brief written plan to change the things you have observed in yourself.

Step 6—Task 5: 5 Problem Areas

My 5 Biggest Problem Areas are:

Problem 1: _____

    To correct this I must: _____

_____

Problem 2: _____

    To correct this I must: _____

_____

Problem 3: _____

    To correct this I must: _____

_____

Problem 4: _____

    To correct this I must: _____

_____

Problem 5: _____

    To correct this I must: _____

_____

Chapter 10
Kindness—Step 7

Who do people say you are? This is a key question asked of Jesus' disciples in the Bible, and one we can ask ourselves. Several scriptures detail the event.

> Jesus and his disciples went on to the villages around Caesarea Philippi. On the way he asked them, "Who do people say I am?" [28] They replied, "Some say John the Baptist; others say Elijah; and still others, one of the prophets." [29] "But what about you?" he asked. Foundation Scripture: (Mark 8:27-29) (See also Matthew. 16:13; Luke 9:18)

The disciples tell Jesus what they have heard. The people who had seen and/or experienced His wondrous miracles, heard His teaching and been healed, were everywhere saying, "Jesus is among the greatest of the prophets, and in fact may be one of the dead prophets come back to life!"

Now Jesus turns to those closest to Him. He asked His disciples, "Who do you say I am?" Peter answers. "You are the Christ."

Jesus then turns to instruct His inner circle of men (who did believe) about how to live as disciples and please God. It is here we learn the importance of an intimate relationship with God. For without the personal relationship with God, which is established by faith, what a person does is completely irrelevant. Only through faith and obedience are we transformed. Only through faith and obedience can we honor God in the way we live our lives.

I ask *you*, who do people say *you* are? Does your life, the way you act, or what you say, allow others to see Jesus? Does your life present a true image of God, of who you are in Christ? Or is the image distorted? Does the way you live bring honor to the Father, the Son, and the Holy Spirit?

If others are asked about you, will they speak of you as a follower of Jesus Christ? Will you be called a "Christian," as they were first called in Antioch? (Acts 11:25-26)

The followers of Jesus were called Christians—not because they carried a big sign proclaiming to be such. No, it was because of the way they lived their lives. Everything about them reflected the life of Jesus: their speech, behavior, the way they treated other believers, and their treatment of those outside the church. Everything about them reflected the life of Jesus. It is the same for us. The way we treat our loved ones, and how we approach God or represent Him to others, are to be Christ-like. And one of the most important qualities of the idea behind "Christ-like" is **kindness**.

Kindness is the essence of Step Seven. Living out the Word of God in our lives is shown by our kindness to others. This includes showing kindness to ourselves. This is where we demonstrate our commitment to established goals and walk 'just as' Jesus. At this step in the Victory Ladder, we come to realize that the answer to the question, "Am I my brother's keeper?" is "Yes". We are to seek the best for others, and ourselves. As Christians we must remember that we are now part of God's family and are called to reach out to each other, and to the world. Through the prophet Jeremiah, we have God's take on this:

> [23] This is what the LORD says: "Let not the wise man boast of his wisdom or the strong man boast of his strength or the rich man boast of his riches, [24] but let him who boasts boast about this: that he understands and knows me, that I am the LORD, who exercises kindness, justice and righteousness on earth, for in these I delight," declares the LORD. (Jeremiah 9: 23- 24)

What does it means to walk as a follower of Christ? Or should I ask, how does one walk so that others might say, "there goes a Christian?" **This will happen when our lives reflect Christ.** Paul gives a plan to help us live for God day by day in (Colossians 3:12-17):

> Therefore, as God's chosen people, holy and dearly loved, clothe yourselves with compassion, kindness, humility, gentleness and patience. [13] Bear with each other and forgive whatever grievances you may have against one another. Forgive as the Lord forgave you. [14] And over all these virtues put on love, which binds them all together in perfect unity. [15] Let the peace of Christ rule in your hearts, since as members of one body you were called to peace. And be thankful. [16] Let the word of Christ dwell in you richly as you teach and admonish one another with all wisdom, and as you sing psalms, hymns and spiritual songs with gratitude in your hearts to God. [17] And whatever you do, whether in word or deed, do it all in the name of the Lord Jesus, giving thanks to God the Father through him.

Can you picture it? As you go about your day and you've taken the word of Christ within your heart, you can rightly divide it as you teach and admonish; or gently make correction when needed, doing all with wisdom, praising and glorifying God. It is in that day you will hear the crowd say, "There is a Christian." "There stands a follower of Christ." This is true for us when we do as Jesus did.

The essence is in the way we treat one another. We are instructed to live in peace with each other as much as possible. This doesn't mean there won't be disagreements or differences of opinion. But if we're walking in love we will work together despite our differences.

I remember the professor of my Hebrew class who told us that when the Rabbis and Scholars in Israel discuss the Scriptures, they may disagree about a particular interpretation and may strongly defend their position, even to the point of pounding on the table. Watching it, you would think they were going to come to blows. However, this practice is considered a form of worship. When they finish, they walk away with no ill feeling toward one another.

However, here in America, how often do we see on television or read of someone fighting as a result of disagreement or, someone killed during a dispute in the name of God? How many churches have been split, or destroyed, because someone didn't agree with the way things were done? Our culture seems to have an attitude that says, "I'm right and you are wrong. It's my way or no way." This is not walking in love. No, God's Word speaks of love in a much different way. Amen! As Christians, we have been called to walk in a love that reflects 1 Corinthians (13:1-8).

Love such as this is not a feeling, but a decision we make to meet others' needs. To reach out with the love of Christ, and minister healing to those who are broken. To offer life to one dying, hope to one feeling hopeless, forgiveness to one bound up in hurt and bitterness, and peace where there is anger and hatred. This means you need to extend this same kindness to yourself.

A commitment to walk in love toward others and ourselves will lead to peace between individuals, loved ones, and among the members of the Body of Christ as a whole. If you have problem relationships that cause conflict, or perhaps complete separation, I urge you to consider in your heart, what you can do to heal those relationships with, and through, the Love of God.

Our heart is the center of conflict because our feelings and desires; our fears and hopes; distrust and trust; jealousy and love; all clash. But, we are admonished to let Christ's peace rule in our hearts. What will the result be when we make a decision to change the way we think and act toward others?

> ⁸Finally, brothers, whatever is true, whatever is noble, whatever is right, whatever is pure, whatever is lovely, whatever is admirable—if anything is excellent or praiseworthy—think about such things. ⁹Whatever you have learned or received or heard from me, or seen in me—put it into practice. And the God of peace will be with you. (Philippians 4:8-9)

Rightness, purity, and acting noble also relate to the way we treat the non-believer. The Church cannot have barriers of nationality, race, education, social standing, wealth, gender, religion, or power. Jesus did away with any walls that man had erected to divide. Was there any greater wall that existed between the Jew and the Gentle? Even that wall had to come down, and was destroyed through the blood of Jesus. (Ephesians 2:11-14)

Alleluia! Every barrier has been broken down through the shed blood of Jesus and all who come to Him are accepted. Not one thing, or any person, should stop you from telling others about Christ or accepting anyone into our fellowship. This includes any, and all, who confess Jesus as Savior and Lord. As Christians, we are called to build bridges, not walls. Again let us remember the words of Romans (5:8): *While we were still sinners, Christ died for us.*

What do we take away from what we've learned here? Simply that as Christians, we are to put on, or clothe ourselves, in Christ-like character.

Yes, we may appear as a strange people—or as the Scriptures say, a "peculiar people" (1 Peter 2:9). As Christians we are to love one another (John 13:34) and carry that love to all, even to the ends of the earth (Acts 1:8). As we continue in the recovery process, we let go of the self-centeredness of our addiction, and reach out with the love of Christ in us. We show kindness to others and also to ourselves.

Being a Christian, showing kindness to others, is not just Christ in you, but Christ living his life through you. Thus, God is glorified when we begin to act in kindness and reflect the love of God.

Step 7 Exercises

There are two tasks for Step 7. The first exercise is about assessing your current relationships. It is similar to a Step Four exercise. This time, you are to assess how these relationships are affecting you positively or negatively. After you have identified how they are affecting you, determine what changes you must make to bring them in line with who you are now.

Step 7—Task 1: Important Relationships in My Life

1. God

My relationship with God in the present: _____

_____

How is my relationship with God influencing my life? _____

_____

How can I improve my relationship with God? _____

_____

What is my goal in this relationship? _____

_____

When will I do this? _____

2. Other person: _____

My relationship to this person: _____

_____

Is this relationship influencing me positively or negatively? _____

What is my goal in this relationship? _____

_____

When will I do this? _____

---

3. Other person: _____

My relationship to this person: _____

_____

Is this relationship influencing me positively or negatively? _____

What is my goal in this relationship? _____

_____

When will I do this? _____

4. Other person: _____

My relationship to this person: _____

_____

Is this relationship influencing me positively or negatively? _____

What is my goal in this relationship? _____

_____

When will I do this? _____

---

5. Other person: _____

My relationship to this person: _____

_____

Is this relationship influencing me positively or negatively? _____

What is my goal in this relationship? _____

_____

When will I do this? _____

Step 7—Task 2: Testimony

The final Step 7 exercise is a verbal Testimony you will make during your group meeting. The topics your testimony should cover include the following:

1. Your current relationship with God, and how knowing God has helped you in recovery.

2. Share at least two examples where you have recognized God working in your life.

3. Include what you have learned about who you are in Christ.

4. Include what you have learned in all the previous steps.

You may make make some notes for yourself below. You may refer to these notes during the testimony, but you cannot just read the notes for the testimony.

NOTES

_____

_____

_____

_____

_____

_____

_____

_____

_____

_____

Chapter 11

Love—Step 8

¹ "I am the true vine, and my Father is the gardener. ² He cuts off every branch in me that bears no fruit, while every branch that does bear fruit he prunes so that it will be even more fruitful. ³ You are already clean because of the word I have spoken to you. ⁴ Remain in me, and I will remain in you. No branch can bear fruit by itself; it must remain in the vine. Neither can you bear fruit unless you remain in me.

⁵ "I am the vine; you are the branches. If a man remains in me and I in him, he will bear much fruit; apart from me you can do nothing. ⁶ If anyone does not remain in me, he is like a branch that is thrown away and withers; such branches are picked up, thrown into the fire and burned. ⁷ If you remain in me and my words remain in you, ask whatever you wish, and it will be given you. ⁸ This is to my Father's glory, that you bear much fruit, showing yourselves to be my disciples.

⁹ "As the Father has loved me, so have I loved you. Now remain in my love. ¹⁰ If you obey my commands, you will remain in my love, just as I have obeyed my Father's commands and remain in his love. ¹¹ I have told you this so that my joy may be in you and that your joy may be complete. (John 15:1-11)

Remember in Step Six we learned that we are to be *just as* Jesus: "imitators; to seek to follow the example of; take as one's model or pattern, to act the same as; impersonate; mimic, to reproduce in form, color, etc., make a duplicate or copy of, to be or become like in appearance; resemble." Here, He tells us to bear fruit—to the Fathers' glory, to remain in Christ and His love for us, and to obey His Word. If we do these things, He will meet our needs and we will know the joy of the Lord. In fact, our joy will be complete.

Circle of Love

Jesus goes on to say:

> [12] My command is this: Love each other as I have loved you. [13] Greater love has no one than this, that he lay down his life for his friends. [14] You are my friends if you do what I command. [15] I no longer call you servants, because a servant does not know his master's business. Instead, I have called you friends, for everything that I learned from my Father I have made known to you.
>
> [16] You did not choose me, but I chose you and appointed you to go and bear fruit—fruit that will last. Then the Father will give you whatever you ask in my name. [17] This is my command: Love each other. (John 15:12-17)

At this point in our journey out of addictions and into Victory, we add **love** to what we say, think, and do. Everything is now placed in God's hands. No longer are we doing things only for ourselves. Now we are willing and able to stop the self-centeredness, writing our own story in life, and the lying and manipulation in our life. (Ephesians 4:15)

Our thoughts, that stinkin'-thinkin', our obsessions, are no longer controlling us. Now we can choose to follow what Paul says in Philippians (4:8-9).

Thus, our actions line up with the Word of God. As we have experienced the Love of God throughout our journey up to Walking in Victory, we now demonstrate that we are followers of Jesus Christ. Our identity of who we are in Christ is now incorporated into our lives. It empowers us to imitate Jesus- not only loving others, but ourselves as well. Paul puts it in perspective in his letter to the Philippians:

> [1] If you have any encouragement from being united with Christ, if any comfort from his love, if any fellowship with the Spirit, if any tenderness and compassion, [2] then make my joy complete by being like-minded, having the same love, being one in spirit and purpose. [3] Do nothing out of selfish ambition or vain conceit, but in humility consider others better than yourselves. [4] Each of you should look not only to your own interests, but also to the interests of others. [5] Your attitude should be the same as that of Christ Jesus. (Philippians 2:1-4)

This may seem like a tall order. You may be asking, "how do I love others, or myself?" You may feel that you have never really felt unconditional love before, let alone truly felt capable of loving someone else. Now you can choose to put all that behind you, and add love to your walk, because, as was stated earlier, God always takes the first step, and then He always walks with you. We know how to love, because He first loved us.

(1 John 4:7-12): _____

_____

_____

_____

_____

_____

_____

_____

_____

_____

Adding love to our walk may be the most difficult step so far. It requires you to expose yourself to hurts, disappointments, and pain. It means to feel emotions you haven't felt in a long time or have suppressed. It requires you to step out into everyday life, and into practicing what is inside of you now—the Love of God.

So here's a question for you. Are You a Face in the Crowd or just a face that is seen?

> [7] Now if the ministry that brought death, which was engraved in letters on stone, came with glory, so that the Israelites could not look steadily at the face of Moses because of its glory, fading though it was, [8] will not the ministry of the Spirit be even more glorious? [9] If the ministry that condemns men is glorious, how much more glorious is the ministry that brings righteousness! [10] For what was glorious has no glory now in comparison with the surpassing glory. [11] And if what was fading away came with glory, how much greater is the glory of that which lasts!
>
> [12] Therefore, since we have such a hope, we are very bold. [13] We are not like Moses, who would put a veil over his face to keep the Israelites from gazing at it while the radiance was fading away. [14] But their minds were made dull, for to this day the same veil remains when the old covenant is read. It has not been removed, because only in Christ is it taken away. [15] Even to this day when Moses is read, a veil covers their hearts. [16] But whenever anyone turns to the Lord, the veil is taken away.
>
> [17] Now the Lord is the Spirit, and where the Spirit of the Lord is, there is freedom. [18] And we, who with unveiled faces all reflect the Lord's glory, are being transformed into his likeness with ever-increasing glory, which comes from the Lord, who is the Spirit. (2 Corinthians. 3:7-18)

We want to focus on verse eighteen. Have you taken the veil off so others can see the Glory of the Lord through you as you go about everyday life? Or are you wearing a veil hiding God's glory?

In Exodus (34:34) we find that when Moses entered the Lord's presence, he removed his veil. This veil was to hide Moses' face, which radiated with the Glory of the Lord. It was so brilliant that the Israelites could not look upon Moses' face as he walked among them. In fact, if you look at the Scripture, you will notice that it is after Moses spoke to the people concerning the Laws of God, that Moses placed the veil over his head.

While he spoke to them, Moses did not need the veil to cover his face, even though they were afraid. When the people had been given the Word of God and Moses was going about his every day duties among them, they could not bear to look at him. It was too much for them to have to look at him.

Aren't we like that at times? We ask for God's help or direction, and then when it comes to walking it out in our everyday lives, we hide the Glory of the Lord that is in us from those with whom we interact. Maybe after church and having just experienced the Glory of God, or having felt His presence, you leave that place and no one can tell any difference in you. You're just a face that is seen.

The Word of God tells us that Moses was unaware of the fact that his face glowed with the Glory of God (Exodus 34:29). Moses did not focus on his appearance, unlike many of us, who are so worried we might offend someone by speaking the name of Jesus in public. Or, who are afraid what someone will think of us if we share the Gospel in a public place. Some of us are so afraid, that we don't openly share the gospel of our Lord and Savior, because we might be rejected. But do you view Moses as fearful? He earlier told God to send someone else. (Exodus 4:13) He is now unaware of the glory of God radiating all over him.

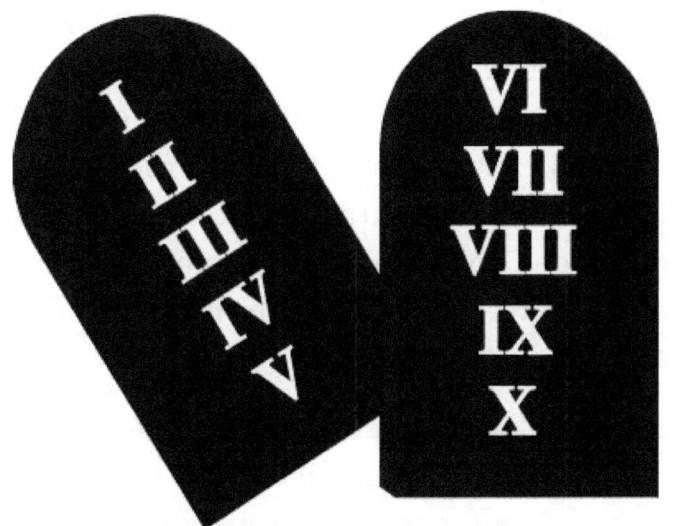

Moses came down from the mountain of God, and gathered the people to bring them the commandments. That was what God had called him to do, and he was just going about the Father's business—he was to bring the Word of God to God's people.

In the Old Testament, Moses had to remove the veil. We learn from our foundation Scripture that the Glory that shown on Moses' face was a fading radiance. It was not going to be present forever. If the Israelites would just wait, they would not have to contend with God's Glory.

However, as a believer, under the New Covenant, it is the Holy Spirit who removes the veil. According to 2 Corinthians (3:18), in the believers' face, the glory of God is reflected. Our relationship with God is eternal. The Lord's abiding presence is permanent, it's not going away. Alleluia! He said he would never leave us, nor forsake us. And that means His glory. Saints, His glory is ever-lasting, and it will take you through whatever trials you have, or anything that the enemy tries to throw at you. Amen!

Satan cannot penetrate the Glory—absolutely not. To the contrary, it is the radiating light of God's glory shining through us that has the power to dispel all darkness. Darkness does not overcome light. Light overcomes darkness. Light is not the absence of darkness, darkness is the absence of light. You see that truth in everyday life. Go into a darkened room and turn on the faintest of light and there is no longer darkness. It has been penetrated by the light. Amen!

It is the same way with us. When we walk in the light of the glory of God, we show the love of God that is in us, and let the Holy Spirit remove the veil. We dispel the darkness around us and let others see Jesus in us. Moses removed the veil when in the presence of God. As we walk in the presence of God we are to walk unveiled. That is the message from God to us today.

Look again at verse 18 in 2 Corinthians. It is with unveiled faces. It says that we *reflect* His glory. The phrase means to reflect, as in a mirror's reflection. The mirrors of that time were made of polished metal, and they reflected images with great brilliance and distinction. That is the truth for us today. Let others see Jesus in us with great brilliance and distinction. Amen!

God isn't finished with us there. We are being *met-am-or-fo'-o* (the Greek word meaning, to *transform* (literally or figuratively metamorphose): change, transfigure, transform. We are being transformed into the likeness of Jesus. That's right! We, one day, will be just as He is (1 John 3:2)! But Saints, that transformation into His likeness began at the cross, and is happening now, and brings a freedom *NOW* that is found in **NO** other way. Amen! Because of the work of Christ on the cross, because of the precious shed blood of Jesus, we have been set free.

We were once enslaved to sin, to the attacks of Satan, and to all forms of bondage—drugs, alcohol, lust, food, sex, and fear to name a few. Now the ever-present, radiant glory of God is continually transforming us to be the exact image of Jesus. As we let that light shine out, the darkness that hides the Truth from so many will be dispelled.

Those who are still enslaved by the things of this world can only find true freedom in knowing the "Truth." Amen! When they know the "Truth," they will be set free and where the Spirit of the Lord is, "there is freedom." Alleluia! When you are free, you do not have to live in fear of anything, or anyone. You can tell the world the good news of Jesus Christ. According to Philippians (4:7), you can walk in a peace that is beyond understanding. You then can love others and yourself.

You understand that we are all molded by the people we associate with, and by our environment. God's Word tells us in 1 Corinthians (15:33): ———————

We can become entwined in the lives of those with whom we have social contact. We, at times, take on the opinions, copy the habits, imitate the manners, and even follow the ritual or customs of those with whom we have daily contact with. In recovery we are asked to change our playmates, playthings, and playgrounds.

This is sound advice. However, as a child of God it does not mean you don't minister the Love of God. Love others, so they may also share in His power and authority.

The "world" says "do not talk of this Jesus." Religion is a private matter. Don't bring God into our schools. Christians are now saying, "I'm a Christian, but that doesn't mean I have to attend church. I believe in Jesus, but I don't need to talk about Him in public. I don't want to be offensive to anyone. We are afraid we might be rejected."

But Saints, just as Jesus came down from the cross, you have been brought down from the cross—just as Moses came down with the Glory of the Lord shining from his face. You, in whatever darkness you're in, as a child of God, I want you to know, He has brought you into his presence where you can stand boldly with an unveiled face. Because you are being transformed, you can transform the world around you. We can demonstrate the Love of God.

Whatever place God has you in, whomever God places in your path, you can shine. When you let the Glory of Lord—His love—radiate, you reflect Christ in you. Your world will no longer be in darkness. It will be transformed to reflect the glory of God.

As an illustration, let me tell you of an episode of *Touched by an Angel*. In this episode, two teenage boys are competing in Olympic trials. They are the best of friends. In fact, they live in the same household, virtually as brothers. This is because when they were kids, one of them lost his parents in a fire that most likely was started by the boys. They had been smoking in the basement and almost got caught. But they ran, and later the house burned down with the parents inside.

The boy who lost his parents then went to live with his best friend and his family. Both boys are then trained by the father to ski. Both are very good at the sport. But one of the boys always wins and the other loses by only a fraction of time. What we learn as the story unfolds, is that the boy who always finishes second, actually was allowing the other one to win. He did this because he felt sorry for his friend, and the loss of his parents.

Because of a tragic accident, the boy who was always the winner, was unable to ever ski again. He asked the other boy to help him die. He couldn't live with his inability to ski. His friend then contemplates whether or not to assist the other boy. One of the angels (Monica), appears to him. Monica convinces him to not help his friend die and says something to him that I want you to consider.

Remember, this boy believed he owed something to the other boy and always let him win. But by doing this he restricted himself to never be all that he could be. No one else could see him as he really was. Monica says to him, "They believed you were the person you appeared to be."

Who do you appear to be to others? In who you are, do others see the LOVE of Jesus? Are you a Face in the crowd or just a face that is seen?

Step 8 Exercise

Step 8 has just one exercise. Your responses to it are shared in group. It is similar to an earlier exercise you did. But since some time has passed, and you have grown in spiritual ways, your responses will be somewhat different.

Step 8—With God/Without God

In this exercise you are to first identify five situations since entering this program where you can see that God was working in your life. Take your time doing this. Try to look over the past few months and find the most significant times you can see you and God working together. Describe them below.

1. _____
2. _____
3. _____
4. _____
5. _____

Next, you are to identify the five situations, or issues, that you still have not surrendered to God (i.e. on your own). Take your time with this. Describe them below.

1. _____
2. _____
3. _____
4. _____
5. _____

Now, consider the times with God in your life. What was the outcome of these situations? Who else was involved? How did you feel toward others and God? What feelings did you experience? How were you co-operating with God?

Now, consider the times in your life where you were not working with God. What was it like not working with God? Who else was involved? How did you feel toward others and God? What feelings did you experience? Use the next page for notes regarding these questions.

Chapter 12
Walking in Love—Step 9

The name of the LORD is a strong tower; the righteous run to it and are safe. (Prov. 18:10)

You have reached the top rung of the Victory Ladder. This is where we are talking the talk and walking the walk. This is where you are now walking in the grace of God, and making choices at the level of grace. You now are doing the right thing because it is the right thing to do. You have gotten to the place that God intended from the beginning. At this level, you will be choosing from right and wrong, not what is right or wrong. In this, you will glorify God in everything you think, say, or do. This is "Walking in Love."

Your climb out of your addiction may have been overwhelming at times. You may have occasionally slid back. But if you're at this step, you are ready to fully trust God and walk in victory.

Trusting in God brings safety! You are safe and secure to live a clean and sober life, to rebuild healthy relationships and establish new ones. Now you can understand that the entire journey has always been about relationships, your relationship with God, others, and yourself. You have a new identity. No longer are you "just an addict," "alcoholic," or any other negative label you have taken on as an identity. You are now a child of God who struggles with these issues, but knows the One Who frees you from the bondages of addiction.

In the Word of God we see that God changed the name of a person to reflect a change in purpose or character. In other words, a person's name was given, or changed, to reflect the individual himself.

In Genesis (17:5) Abram (exalted father) became Abraham (father of many). In (verse 15) of that same chapter, Abraham is no longer to call his wife Sarai. She will be called Sarah, be blessed with a son, and be the mother of many nations. Even kings shall come from her.

We also read of Saul, who becomes the apostle to the Gentiles, is called Paul in Acts (13:9). In John (15:15) Jesus says, we are now called "friend."

In ancient Judaism, "name" often meant reputation or renowned, it was who the person was. In 1 John (2:12) when God acted, He was defending his honor. When one spoke, he or she spoke as God's representative, thus acting on His behalf. (Exodus 5:23).

> If anyone does not listen to my words that the prophet speaks in my name, I myself will call him to account. [20] But a prophet who presumes to speak in my name anything I have not commanded him to say, or a prophet who speaks in the name of other gods, must be put to death." [21] You may say to yourselves, "How can we know when a message has not been spoken by the LORD?" [22] If what a prophet proclaims in the name of the LORD does not take place or come true, that is a message the LORD has not spoken. That prophet has spoken presumptuously. Do not be afraid of him. (Deuteronomy 18:19-22)

Remember in Acts where Peter and John are confronted by the crippled man at the temple gate? He asked Peter and John for money. However, not having money to give, Peter speaks for them and says, (Acts 3:6):

_____

_____

_____

_____

_____

The man got up and was healed. Peter and John were acting on behalf of God. They were speaking in the name or authority of God, as if God were right there.

When praying, to call on a deity's name simply meant addressing him. An example is at Mount Carmel, when Elijah tells the 450 Prophets of Baal to prepare their sacrifice, and then tells them:

> Then you call on the name of your god, and I will call on the name of the LORD. The god who answers by fire—he is God." Then all the people said, "What you say is good." (1 Kings 18:24)

In New Testament times, a person's name stood for the person. In John (17:6, 26), the *New International Version Bible* translates the Greek "Your name" by the word "You."

Thus, we can understand that when we speak the phrase, "the name of the Lord," we are speaking of His person. We are speaking of Him specifically. That is, we are speaking of His character and qualities. The very nature of God is in His Name.

In Exodus (3:14-15); we see that the name of God is His covenant name by which he made Himself known to His people:

> God said to Moses, "I AM WHO I AM. This is what you are to say to the Israelites: 'I AM has sent me to you.'" ¹⁵ God also said to Moses, "Say to the Israelites, 'The LORD, the God of your fathers—the God of Abraham, the God of Isaac and the God of Jacob—has sent me to you.' This is my name forever, the name by which I am to be remembered from generation to generation.

Scripture tells us who "I AM WHO I AM" is. Read the following passages and write what you learn of God.

(Genesis 14:18): _____

(Genesis 16:13): _____

(Genesis 21:33): _____

(Psalm 28:7): _____

(Psalm 37:39): _____

(Psalm 142:5): _____

(Genesis 22:14): _____

(Isaiah 5:16):_____

This is the God who first loved us, and the God who sent His Son that we might have life more abundantly; that we may know what true love is; that we are the head and not the tail; that we would be prosperous; that all our needs would be met; that we may know God, and be one with Him through Jesus Christ; and that we have all authority over the enemy.

God is not a man; therefore, He cannot lie, because He is faithful, because our Lord and Savior prayed before He went to be with the Father:

> I will remain in the world no longer, but they are still in the world, and I am coming to you. Holy Father, protect them by the power of your name—the name you gave me—so that they may be one as we are one. ¹²While I was with them, I protected them and kept them safe by that name you gave me. None has been lost except the one doomed to destruction so that Scripture would be fulfilled. (John 17:11-12)

We can be assured of His protection, and that in His name we are safe. When we put our whole trust in Him and run into His arms, we are then safe in Him. And we can be confident and safe when we take refuge in the covenant Name of God. The great I AM is our strong tower. Amen!

For us, God is a strong tower, a refuge, a place where we may turn for safety. He is our source of strength when the world seems to come down around us, when all seems to be lost, when you feel that there is no hope. When you feel that you have no strength left to fight or continue in recovery, He is there as a strong tower to provide a safe refuge, Glory to God! Amen!

Let me remind you here. The Hebrew word used in Proverbs (18:10) is *saw-gab;* meaning, "to be inaccessible," and by implication, "safe, strong." What God is saying is that when we trust in Him and we walk in His name we are literally made too strong to be overcome by any addiction, the things of this world, or the attacks of the enemy.

The truth of Proverbs (18:10) is this: When we understand that trust in the *name of the* LORD is trusting in the Lord Himself. That He is the Protector of the righteous. He takes His children and makes them safe in Himself, and lifts them above the danger. Alleluia!

You can then stand safe, as a child of God who walks in the name of the Lord, and puts your trust in Him as your strong tower. Another way of saying it is, "I am too strong to be brought down." Amen! Let's make a comparison of two lives to see this.

Look at Judas Iscariot, when he saw that Jesus had been condemned, he was overwhelmed with remorse. He couldn't live with himself ,and even tried to return the thirty pieces of silver. But the chief priests and elders would have nothing to do with him. What Judas did next tells us what his understanding was of the grace of God. We see that he did not see God as a refuge, someone to turn to in his anguish and sin.

With no one to turn to, Judas runs away and commits suicide. He had been with Jesus for three years, knew the One who was his strength, his strong tower, but did not know that he could run to Jesus and be forgiven, and be safe in His arms.

Now, look at David's life. When he was confronted with his sins, he knew in his heart that God's grace was greater than any sin or problem he faced. How do we remember David? Not as an adulterer or murderer. No. We remember him as a man after God's own heart (Acts 13:22). David knew that nothing he did or needed was too hard for God to handle. David sang of this in Psalm (9:9-10).

Our being safe does not depend on anything we have done, not on our own wisdom, or on our own strength. It is because of God's love for his children.

David declares God's view toward us in Psalm (27:5): _____

_____

_____

_____

And that rock is Jesus Christ. And if Jesus is Lord of my life, then I am, (Colossians 3:3-4):

_____

_____

_____

_____

I no longer have to fight the enemy or worry about life's trials. I only need to seek the safety of being hidden in Christ. When I am hidden in Christ, I no longer have to carry the load.

I trust Jesus to be my strength, my fortress. I know Him as my advocate. I am able to stand strong in recovery.

When we trust in the Lord and run to Him in time of need, instead of seeking to handle life in our own strength, writing our own story, we can than say as David said:

> Then my head will be exalted above the enemies who surround me; at his tabernacle will I sacrifice with shouts of joy; I will sing and make music to the LORD. (Psalm 27:6)

And we can shout (Proverbs 18:10): _____

_____

_____

_____

Do you know how serious God takes this? He takes it so serious that in Zechariah (2:8-9) we hear the words of Zechariah in speaking to the Jew in exile:

> ⁸ For this is what the LORD Almighty says: "After he has honored me and has sent me against the nations that have plundered you—for whoever touches you touches the apple of his eye—I will surely raise my hand against them so that their slaves will plunder them. Then you will know that the LORD Almighty has sent me.

Do you hear that? When it seems that everything is against you, when the enemy tries to kill, steal or destroy you, it's as if these attacks were directly against God. In everyday language, when you mess with me, you are messing with my Father.

When the enemy comes against you and the world gets you down, when life has you surrounded by its trials and temptation, when you find that you have no strength to go on, when you are wondering where your next meal will come from or you are down to your last dollar, or you are down to your last dollar, or when you feel the urge to drink or graving to use, it is to Christ we turn. Yes cry out, "Lord: Keep me as the apple of your eye; hide me in the shadow of your wings." (Psalm 17:8) Alleluia! Amen!

Saints, picture in your mind, and get it deep into your heart. Just as a mother bird builds her nest high in a tree to protect her young from harm, and as the young birds find shelter and safety under the shadow of their mother's wings; if we trust in God and run to Him, we will find safety and strength in His arms.

Not in our strength, trying to prove how tough we are, but strengthened in the power of God to repair broken relationships. To rid ourselves of resentments. To stay clean and sober. This is the step where we want to live, walking with the Father. It is here that we know God's love: "And this is love: that we walk in obedience to his commands. As you have heard from the beginning, his command is that you walk in love." (2 John 1:6).

You will now put into action all that you have learned through your journey up the Victory Ladder, to Walking in love. The truths you have learned need to be practiced every day. If you find yourself going back down the ladder, return to the step that gets you back on track, toward the top. Walk in His G. R. A. C. E. (God's Riches at Christ's Expense).

Walk in Victory

Final Program Exercise

Your final exercise is to give back to the group. We ask you to give a few words of encouragement to those that have not completed this phase of their recovery. Remember, you are a Christian role model. The words you choose to say may have a profound impact on your fellow Christians and group members.

> Do your best to present yourself to God as one approved, a workman who does not need to be ashamed and who correctly handles the word of truth. (2 Timothy 2:15)

About the Author

Bob and his wife have been married for over forty-four years. He holds a Master of Arts degree in Christian Counseling and a Bachelor of Arts degree in Pastoral Care and Church Administration with a minor in counseling from Oral Roberts University. He is presently a Licensed Alcohol & Drug Counselor, an International Certified Advanced Alcohol & Drug Counselor, and a Board Approved Supervisor for CADC candidates. He is trained at the advanced level of Moral Reconation Therapy in Substance Abuse and Domestic Violence.

He is an ordained minister of the Gospel and has served as a pastor, and as a Pastor of Counseling. He has been an Adjunct Professor at Oklahoma Wesleyan University, Bacone College and guest lecturer for graduate and doctoral level classes at Oral Roberts University. He was executive director of an outpatient alcohol and drug center for over eight years in Bartlesville, Oklahoma. He owned and operated Harvest Counseling Center in Bartlesville, Oklahoma for 12 years.

He served 12 years in the United States Air Force. He was one of the first thirty-one counselors selected to test for advanced certification within ICRC in Oklahoma and be certified. He has served as past president of Washington County Association for Mental Health. He is a charter member of the American Association of Christian Counselors and a member of International Christian Coaching Association.

He currently is in private practice and focusing on writing and ministering the Gospel through counseling, life coaching, and preaching.

NOTES

NOTES

NOTES